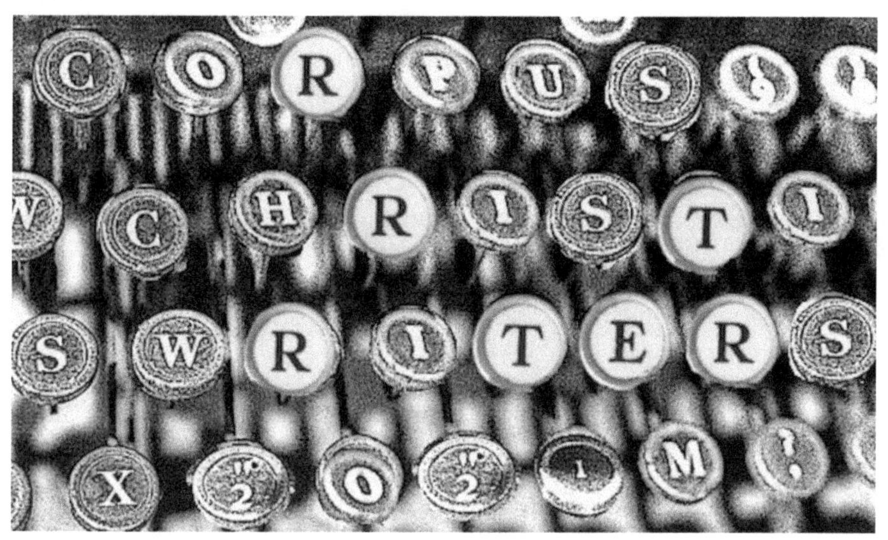

CORPUS CHRISTI WRITERS 2021

Edited by
William Mays

Any resemblance to actual events, locales, or persons, either living or dead, in this anthology is purely coincidental.

For more information contact
William Mays
Mays Publishing.
Books@mayspublishing.com

Cover Photo by Mrinal Gosain

Title Page Photo by Dave Lynch
Additional Title Page Keys by William Mays

Cover Design by Alexis Mays Harborth

Marketing Manager Alexis Mays Harborth

Copy Editor Tom Murphy

Promotional Photo Belinda Aguilar

Special Thanks to Joseph Wilson

Printed in the United States of America

ISBN 978-1-7334696-3-0

Introduction

Corpus Christi Writers strives to present diverse views and perspectives that, taken as a whole, reflect what people in this community are thinking. Many writers from previous anthologies return to this fourth book in the series, and many new writers join them. Youthful exuberance coexists with polished style. Chupacabras reappear. Talking animals take a hiatus, but the chatty squirrel will not be denied. People who live on the edge share time and space with those who support traditional values. Surprisingly, there are no stories of a dystopian future, but the search for love and meaning remains universal—and elusive. Some strive for sexual identity; others find passion in unexpected places; a few accept isolation and self-reliance. Sometimes, a harsh physical environment tests one's mettle and underscores internal conflict.

Visuals play an essential role in this book, sometimes as annotations to the writing, sometimes integrated into the works. Standalone images illustrate the writing process.

This anthology features a group project. While seemingly silly, it touches on serious topics such as fake news and the spoofing of websites.

You can find more information about the writers at MaysPublishing.com. You will also find many other stories and poems from writers from around the world. We urge you to submit your work. MaysPublishing.com also features galleries of the artists and photographers who contribute to our projects.

Thanks to all who participated. We feel there is great talent here, and we appreciate the opportunity to showcase it.

...

Table of Contents

Images

FIRST LINES by William Mays

ALAN BERECKA

Alan Berecka was the Poet Laureate of Corpus Christi from February 2017 - February 2019. Berecka earns his keep as a reference librarian at Del Mar College. His work has appeared in such publications as *Red River Review*, *Texas Review*, *The Christian Century*, *Windhover*, *Ruminate*, *St. Peter's B-List* and *Oklahoma Poems...And Their Poets*.

The Great Escape

"He needs to find a job."
My boozy mother's voice
echoed throughout
our cabin-sized house
as she worked at the stove
frying breaded pork chops.
"What the hell for? We ain't broke"
My father home from his shift
at the sheet metal shop,
covered in sweat and grime
sat in the kitchen unlacing
his Redwing high tops, his beer
sweating a ring to his side
as it waited on the table.
"It'll be good for him.
He's not doing a damn thing
this summer, let him learn
some responsibility?" "Stella,
I've been working like a dog
since I was fourteen. It ain't taught
me didley about squat yet." "Albert
it's time he does some growing up."
"Stella, he's got one year of school
left. Let him enjoy it. He'll be working
the rest of his life. Three months
flipping burgers can't buy anything
better than time." She let the argument
drop. I sat on my bed, book in hand,
smiling, grateful for the reprieve.

Skeletons

As a kid I always found it harsh
when my mother claimed that if given
the chance, she'd become a cloistered nun.

My father, an old dog, loved to roll
in life's dirt. One night after I graduated
from high school, my bags packed for college,
he swayed up to me, a fresh Manhattan
sweating and sloshing in his hand. He offered
me slurred advise. Kid, ya know if I could
do it all over again, I'd be an effing pimp.

After returning from my semester abroad,
I handed out souvenirs. I gave my mom
water from Lordes, a rosary blessed
by the Pope and a cheap t-shirt. I brought
my dad brandy from Spain, a Hofbrau-
haus half-liter stein, and second hand
accounts of his WWII Pig Alley haunts.

My mother enjoyed her gifts, especially
her John Paul II shirt. He stood arms raised
and spread, glowing in black and white.
That it was two sizes too large didn't matter
to her. She wore it often and took to saying
again and again, I can't believe how happy
the Pope looks. My father, who believed
only to a certain point, finally broke one night
at our family meal. To her constant refrain,
he shot back, For Christ sake, Stella,
I'd be ecstatic too if I had a tit in each hand.
My mother looked down. The Pope looked
up smiling, her breasts resting in his open palms.
She said nothing. I brayed and snorted, laughing
along with my bent and breathless dad.

A few days later, the shirt appeared, hanging
neatly in the corner of my closet. I didn't wear
it much and never in my mother's presence.

ALISA HOPE WAGNER

Alisa Hope Wagner is an award-winning author, editor and publisher of over 30 books. She married her high school sweetheart, and together they raise their three children in a Christ-centered home.

Breaking the Religious Spirit
Illustration by Albert Morales

Promises too lofty for me to reach.
Underserving. Lacking. Never enough.

What can I fix?
What can I change?
What can I learn?
What can I erase?

Analyzing,
Repenting,
Striving,
Condemning,
Self-loathing –
Never enough.

Joy vanishes behind self-righteousness.
Peace dissolves behind discouragement.

The enemy creeps in.
Makes a home in my pain.
And a bed in my fear.
Builds a system of torment in my mind.

Promises too lofty for me to reach.
Damnation punctures my heart.
My soul bleeds out.
And death replaces hope.

Demons laugh and lie.
I listen. I examine. Nothing computes.
The racket rages around me.
My inner screams can't compete.

"Quiet yourself," He gently whispers.

No! No! The lies slice!

"Quiet yourself," He repeats.

It hurts! Make them stop!

Where is Your Peace?
Where is Your Joy?
Where are Your Promises?

"Trust me. And quiet yourself."

The lies blare on as I sit silently.
Each like an old record, spinning the evil noise.
Louder and louder until the clashing becomes
A single static whine.

"What do you hear?" He asks.

I sense it now, as God sits with me in the shadows.
The lies create distraction,
Desperately disguising a singular truth:
Satan's seething, supernatural aversion for me.

he hates my design by God.
he hates my destiny from God.
he hates my dependency on God.

Discouragement begets condemnation.
Condemnation begets lies.
And lies beget death.

I'm dismantling the system of torment.
Piece by putrid piece.
Lie by vile lie.
Until joy overwhelms self-righteousness.
And peace overshadows discouragement.

Promises are too lofty.
But they are gifts for me.
I can't earn them.
I can only believe.

Finally, my striving dies in the arms of faith.
Jesus is enough.

Killing Perfection

I'm losing her

Childhood moments mourn
While secrets shade the soul
Can't confess to perfection
Striving steals a mother's role

Listen to what she wants
Switch to a secular station
Young hearts yearn to cry
To songs without redemption

Love can't conceal the world
And perfection fails at saving
Produces patterns of shame
With safe towers suffocating

Mistakes move adolescence
Life's troubles slide into view
Trade fear for freedom of failing
Sheltered safeguards devastate too

Canceling my own condemnation
Merry mistakes no longer hide
Grace unites my daughter to me
As perfection commits suicide

I'm finding her

The Alphabet of Jesus

My Award.
My Best.
My Clarity.
My Divinity.
My Energy.
My Freedom.
My God.
My Healing.
My Integrity.
My Joy.
My Kindness.
My Love.
My Miracle.
My Nobility.
My Obedience.
My Perfection.
My Quiet.
My Redemption.
My Strength.
My Truth.
My Understanding.
My Victory.
My Way.
My Xerox.
My Youth.
My Zeal.

ALLYSON LARKIN

Allyson Chavez Larkin is a family physician specializing in wound care. She reads and writes voraciously in her spare time.

Chupacabra

The school bus sped away in a cloud of dust. Tony started up the steep drive to the ranch house. The afternoon sun baked the back of his neck. His backpack bit into his shoulders and sweat dripped into his eyes.

Tony wiped his face and rolled his neck. He swallowed hard. Ever since his mom died in the car wreck six weeks ago, he felt like he couldn't take a full breath. It was like an invisible hand was wrapped around his throat choking him all day long.

He kicked a rock. It ricocheted off a stump and hit him in the knee. It figured. Tony was mad all the time but couldn't figure out at who. His mother for dying? His father for dishing him off on his grandpa? His grandpa for living so far out in the country that he had to ride the bus an hour to school?

When Tony finally reached the house, he was surprised to see the sheriff's truck parked out front. The sheriff and Tony's grandpa were deep in conversation.

"Two sheep. Completely drained of blood on Wednesday," the sheriff said. "And last night, three calves and Mrs. Smith's Blue Heeler. All dead, with nothing but puncture wounds on their necks."

"No other injuries?" Tony's grandpa asked.

"None." The sheriff shrugged. "It's the darndest thing."

"It's a Chupacabra," Tony's grandpa said. "They've been round these parts before."

The sheriff laughed. "I'd not jump to that conclusion, Mr. Saenz. More likely a cougar wandering out of the mountains. Still, you'd best pen your stock tonight."

Tony's grandpa didn't argue. "Thanks for letting us know."

As soon as the sheriff pulled away, Tony said, "Grandpa, you can't go talking like that. People will think you're crazy."

Grandpa shook his wooly, grey head. "Crazy is denying what's right before your eyes. Cougars eat their prey. They don't suck their blood."

Inside, his grandpa pulled a faded photo from a drawer. It was

Tony's mother. She was about his age and had long brown pigtails and was cradling a baby goat with a pink collar in her arms.

"The Chupacabra killed Lulu, your mother's favorite goat, last time it was round these parts. Your mother cried for days."

Tony walked away. He didn't want to talk about his mother. It felt like the blood was being sucked out of him every time he tried.

After dinner Tony headed outside to round up the goats. Once there had been a whole herd on the ranch. But now his grandpa only kept a nanny, a billy, and a baby goat born last spring.

The baby was black with white patches above each hoof and looked like she'd stepped in a can of paint. She followed Tony around when he did his chores, chewing on his sleeves and begging for treats.

Grandpa had told Tony he could name her, but Tony hadn't. He didn't want to care about a baby goat—or anything else for that matter. Still, he fed her the best scraps and made sure she got her fair share of oats and hay before the bigger goats moved in. At night he brushed her till her coat shined.

The nanny and the billy were dozing under the porch and refused to come out when Tony called. He had to crawl underneath and pull them out by their collars. The billy gave Tony a sharp nip on his hand to show his displeasure, but both were happy enough when Tony filled their troughs with fresh hay and water.

Then, Tony searched the yard for Baby Goat calling and shaking a cupful of Cheerios, but she didn't answer. He walked the entire back pasture, but she wasn't there, either. So he headed down the hill to the meadow by the river, carefully avoiding the family cemetery that stood on its edge.

The meadow had been Tony's favorite spot on the ranch when he was a kid. It was shady and next to the river with a nice fishing hole. But now, since his mother had been buried there, a fresh mound of brown dirt marking the spot; he hated the place. He hadn't fished a single time, even though Grandpa had bought him a new rod and reel.

Tony scoured the underbrush walking up and down the river's edge calling for Baby Goat, but she was nowhere to be seen. He gave up when it was too dark to see.

"Any luck?" Grandpa asked when Tony returned.

Tony shook his head.

Grandpa squeezed Tony's shoulder with his strong, gnarled hand. "She'll wander on home when she's ready."

Tony nodded and headed to bed. He hadn't slept well since his mom died. During the day he could barely hold his eyes open. But at night his brain ran on overdrive replaying memories of his mother.

Grandpa had brought her old comic books and baseball cards down from the attic. Tony pored over them. Baseball was Tony's sport, and his mother had loved it, too. They both played third base. She'd played softball in college and after that on a woman's league. She'd been on her way to a tournament when her car was hit by the tractor trailer.

He was staring at the clock at midnight, when he heard an urgent, high-pitched bleat. He hopped out of bed slipping his bare feet into his boots, grabbed the flashlight on the counter next to the door, and ran outside toward the sound. The cries continued frantic and shrill.

Tony sprinted through the yard and into the pasture wearing only his boxers and boots. Brambles tore his skin, but he didn't slow. The bleating led him to the top of the hill. He hesitated, wondering if he should get his grandpa. But then Baby Goat cried even louder. There was no time.

As he raced down the slope, a cloud passed over the moon. The darkness became so deep, Tony couldn't even see his feet. He stumbled on rocks and ruts but didn't slow. He followed Baby Goat's maws into the meadow then skidded to a stop. The bleating was coming from the cemetery.

He shined his flashlight inside the stone walls, but the thin yellow light couldn't penetrate the thick mist.. It hovered over the ground hugging the tombstones like a living thing. It seemed to breathe.

Tony wanted to help Baby Goat, but his feet were frozen as if chained to the ground. He looked around for someone, anyone, to help him. But he was all alone.

Baby Goat shrieked again, higher now, desperate. The sound made the hairs stand straight up on Tony's arms. But, somehow, released the lock on his feet.

Tony opened the gate and ran inside. A huge beast like a hairless, coyote with thick, grey skin crouched over baby goat pinning her tiny body to the stone wall with a giant paw.

"Get out of here!" Tony yelled.

The beast looked up at Tony with angry yellow cat eyes. Blood dripped from its two long, curved incisors. Tony smashed the beast's muzzle with his flashlight. The beast roared and raised up on its hind legs towering over Tony.

Tony turned and ran. The ground shook as the beast pursued him. He could feel the beast's hot, rancid breath on his neck. It was gaining on him. Tony focused every ounce of his energy into running as fast as he could toward the river praying the beast could not swim.

But barely a foot from the water's edge, the beast roared and leapt onto Tony's back, knocking him to the ground. As he fell he glimpsed a girl running towards him through the mist. She held a baseball bat in front of her like a club.

Then, Tony's head smashed the ground. The beast pierced his neck with its razor incisors. Tony screamed as blood began to flow out of him. In that moment the girl reached them. She struck the beast with her bat. It roared, releasing Tony. The girl whacked the beast again, swinging the bat as if she was hitting a line drive. Tony heard the crack as the bat impacted the beast's skull.

The beast yelped and took off running along the river's edge. The girl knelt next to Tony and pressed her hand against his bleeding neck.

"Don't worry. I'll take care of you."

Tony wondered, briefly, why she seemed so familiar. Then he blacked out.

When Tony came to, light shone through the barn window. His grandpa was crouched over him.

Tony sat up. "Grandpa, how did you get me up the hill?"

"I found you here, just now."

The events of the night rushed back to him. Tony brought his hand to his neck. A thick dressing was taped to his skin.

"Grandpa, a chupacabra killed Baby Goat. And there was a girl—"

"Baby Goat is fine." Grandpa pointed. "She's here with you."

Sure enough, Baby Goat lay curled next to Tony with a bandage on her neck that matched his own. She had a collar, too. It was faded pink but clearly read, "Lulu."

Grandpa sat back on his heels. "Isn't that strange?"

Tony scratched Lulu's chin. She mawed and butted him gently with her baby horns.

Every inch of Tony's body ached, but he didn't care. For the first time since his mother died, the invisible hand had released its grip on his throat. He could breathe again.

ALYANNA MENA

Alyanna Mena is a nursing student in Corpus Christi. Many live to work; however, she works to live. She loves reading, painting, drawing, and singing. Author's note: My family is my life, and I am glad I can share a little bit of what that is. I thank my friends and family for always being there to support me and thank those who have recently departed while keeping them close in my heart.

Candy

What an enticing wrapper
Dried, the rustling cover sounded of leaves
Yet when wet, scarlet bleeds through the delicate paper onto your fingertips

The holder doesn't remember the sweeties' origin other than from their pocket

Your lustful eyes gaze upon my naked body
My clothing crimped in one hand while gripping me softly in another
You place me between your lips and suck the sweet juices

The swirling cinnamon burns the tongue but cools when inhaled
So long as you don't choke

Early evening,

When the sun and the moon pass off shift report as the moon dresses for work.

Being a white night owl, the hue in the sky signals my need for candy. Because within a place, all different sorts of confectionaries await to be swallowed.

Each step on the tile, rhythmic like a heartbeat. The door beeps behind me as the lock engages and I breathe in the cold air perfumed with alcohol.

I study each jar carefully deciding which will fill my craving. As I lift a bottle the soft rattle increases the anticipation as I choose my sweet. My mouth waters like a toddler.

My fingers twist the lid open and I place 3 small red pills onto my palm of my hand. I lick my lips, work has just started.

BRENDA ELAINE RIOJAS

Brenda Riojas is a graduate student at Texas A&M University - Corpus Christi. Her professor and classmates inspired her to create "Broken." During her free time, she enjoys spending time with her parents, brother Ruben, and dog Rufus

Broken

Hello,

Congratulations!
You've found me.

I'll start with my name, and that's Birdie. My father insisted on going against family tradition and not gift me his name. That's what my mother wanted, but she had no choice; she was already dead. I lived the best childhood any kid could ever experience. I had CDs, VCRs, posters, and so many toys. Living my teen years in the 2000s was magical. I had the thinnest eyebrows and wanted to be Britney Spears every morning when I got dressed. I imagined that life would stay like 1998 and never be different. Calling my best friend on our landline and making my daddy mad when I would pick up the other phone while he talked to grandma. The good ole days, right?

Too bad she was never a mother figure but was always there for me. I never once heard from my mother's family; it's like they existed on another planet that wasn't very far away. My life has been normal even without my mother. Her presence has always surrounded me and my father. He knew if he was too close to me and if he lost me one day, it'd be a repeat. We were close, but he always kept a distance.

This bottle is the last one that my father drank out of. He nearly drank himself to death on my mother's anniversary. We longed for her, but now he longed for so much beer. It was his escape, and mine was writing. I wrote my feelings until my pages were soaked. I trash dug this bottle but wiped it clear with my tears and drowned it in my bathtub of sorrows. I tested out this experiment just for you.

I took myself to the beach, the edge of the water, and saw something.

I saw myself on the water, no, not my reflection.

I finally got to see where my tears went. Years of crying and years of mourning.

This morning I placed my hands over my heart and realized enough was enough. I crumbled my paper and attempted to throw it into the water. No bottle, no cork, just paper, and water, soaked like it would be on my desk anyway. This bottle was the last treasure of my father. I now have nothing that belongs to him. I have our memories and now your condolences.

How did you find me? Tell me.
Know that you've found me when I lost myself.
By this time, I've probably found myself again.

Tell me now; scream it to the sky or whisper it in the wind.

Tell me now who you are and how why you broke this bottle in half. Did you think you'd find treasure or money? You actually found a fortune, and that was this wine bottle. My father never drank cheap, and I didn't recover a broken bottle either.

Now, this fortune is worth nothing.

You broke it. It's your fault, but you didn't know that.

A fortune could be even a dollar to anybody, but it's worth memories to me. This was the last memory of my father, his last bottle. Perhaps it's both of our lasts, his last bottle, and my last letter.

Wait, calm down; you aren't in trouble; there aren't any "cLuES" to my mysterious death or to my mysterious "RunAWaY" in this final letter. Because I didn't.

I didn't die or run away.

Well, I guess there's a mystery, and that's why I'm writing as if I'm still here. I decided to find myself and just let go. I let go of my troubles and left them to you.

I had a problem with my childhood home. The one I told you about and the one I grew up in. I treasured that thing because I could go upstairs and smell my mother anytime I wanted at her vanity. I could also play dress-up when my father wasn't looking because he'd just cry, mourn and scream.

I only ask that you save it and bid on it. You better bid big, baby.

Are you broke?
Because you aren't now.
Turn this page over —>

And bid.
Here's my last check and clear my name.

Take care of what was mine like it's yours because it is.

Start over the way that I couldn't.

I wasn't strong enough to live alone in an empty, once-full home.

It's not haunted or ghosted.

My name is still active, and you can live the double life that I wanted.

When you enter, walk ten steps up the stairs, and you'll hear a creak. Trust me; you'll hear a creak on that step. Lift the carpet and get what you can before it's gone. Give yourself time to consider what you want to do. You want to renovate, redecorate, purchase a car? Do it; I'll never know. Just stay off the streets and remain low, lay low and never speed. That's all I did, and now you might pay the price for it.

Do you get it?

Do I need to explain again?

Here I'll sum it up:

My mother died the moment I was born, and my father cared for me. We missed her dearly, and all my father ever did was hope to see her again. He would show me where he'd stand and watch her get ready at her vanity. He told me once to sit there so he could imagine my mother. He cried for days after that, and on the final day, he was gone the same as her twenty years later. I drank and sped up and down the street in frustration. I almost ended up behind bars for it. This was the last letter I ever wrote. I couldn't bear to live to see the date my parents didn't make it to. I couldn't mourn the day of my mother without my father.

Go to my home and buy it. My father never finished paying it, and the government took it. Repurchase it. I can't. I'm not strong enough to start over and begin a life of my own. Why not leave it to a stranger.

Go to the tenth stair and take my cash and identity. Don't be scared, just live. Live the life that I couldn't. You'll find the home looks like I just cleaned and went out to the grocery store and never returned. In other words, it'll feel like home. I snuck in last night and rearranged it the way I remembered it, not the way the realtor wanted it. For the last two weeks, I've unfortunately seen two families look and be interested. This check will let you bid the highest and get to keep my memories safe. Pay off my tickets and carry on. Carry that cash and live November 26 like it was my last because it's your first.

Do you have a husband or wife, maybe a child? Whoever and whatever you are, look at the blueprints under the sink, and you'll find all of the hidden treasures buried in the walls. I stand here twenty-one years later and must follow in my family's footsteps. I don't know any different and not any better. Don't worry about our family coming for you; they're on another planet and think I'm still living my sorry life.

If you don't agree, just rebottle this paper and leave it in the sand, don't throw it into the water because I didn't do that. Make it look like it just came from the water so some other nosy person like you can find it, crack it, and get to live my fortune.

Unlike you,
Birdie E. Lane
(By this time, I'm swimming in my sorrows, floating in my tears, and flying my spirit)

CAROL MAYS

Carol Mays wrote *103 Crazy Ideas for Surviving Suburbia* and co-wrote *Escape from Sunny Shores* with her husband. She also wrote *Nevins*, the story of a talking cat, and the sequel, *Nevins 2: Saving the Junkyard.*

Soapstone Creek

We were not a traditional family with the father having a career and the mom being a housewife. My parents were auctioneers of antiques and collectible junk. We were in a constant state of gathering "stuff," selling it, and then getting more "stuff." We were simply carrying on with the family trade my Italian grandfather started in Rhode Island during the Great Depression.

In 1969 we made a road trip from Corpus Christi to Providence to get more "stuff." My oldest brother (the WWII baby) had already moved out. This left my sister (who is 17 years older than me) and my other brother (who is ten years older than me).

I was three. I remember my potty chair with the teddy bear decal.

We were quite a sight. My dad, who'd fought in the "big one" WWII as a SeaBee, had a huge, two-ton truck that he built sides for with plywood. He painted it white and wrote in black, old English letters: Auction Arena with our name and address on it. The top of the truck was covered with a heavy, green canvas. It clung to the truck and smelled earthy. Ropes, attached to the sides, swung in every direction as we lumbered down the road. The top- heavy truck swayed left to right like a ship at sea, but my father drove it with confidence and purpose. He would shift the gears— something that looked like a long metal stick. I sat next to it. A red button was used for over-drive up the hills. We would shut the engine off and coast down the hills to save gas.

Behind the truck, we pulled a little pop-up trailer that rode on two wheels. My dad bought it cheap at Woolco—the Wal-Mart of its day. We were like gypsies living on the road and setting up camp wherever we could. We never stayed in camp sites. We truly camped, and in 1969 so did the hippies. My father hated the hippies because they burned their draft cards, had long hair, and refused to serve their country as he had. Much later, he appreciated their view of things. But, in 1969, he hated them. And, on this one day, in Selma, Alabama, we stopped driving early and stopped alongside Soapstone Creek.

Colorful trees were all around. I couldn't tell you if it was spring or summer. It could have been early fall. But I can tell you that the weather was perfect. Not too hot. Not too cold. The air was fresh, warm, and earthy. It was beautiful. We poured out of the long, bench-style vinyl seat, my dad on the driver's side, my mother on the passenger side, followed by my sister and brother.

Someone had to help me out. There was no baby seat in those days. My dad made a wooden shelf balanced on the dashboard that hung from two ropes attached to the ceiling of the truck. It was a wooden hammock with a perfect view. Today, this would not be legal, but it was 1969.

My father and brother methodically made their way to the back of the truck to unhitch the trailer. My dad lifted it with Herculean strength, rolled it backward, then my brother cranked it in place to balance it. My dad then got back in the truck to move it up a few feet. He lumbered back to the camper, which he and my brother magically turned into a home. They attached the pipes to the top, and then it folded out. Everything was manual. The green canvas took shape, and that familiar earthy smell greeted us. The camper only had a full-size bed on each side. No bathroom, no kitchen, no conveniences at all. My brother slept in the cab of the truck at night. He loved it. Anxious to swim in the creek, he asked my dad if he could go and explore. Dad, preoccupied with something, muttered, "yeah." My brother took off like a jack rabbit. I could see him wading in the water—his pant legs pushed up over his knees. My mother and sister were setting up the camp stove and chatting away. I stood next to my dad, fascinated by his endless energy to work. I don't know what he was fixing, but whatever it was—it was important. He hammered away, tightened something, and hammered again.

Suddenly, appearing out of nowhere, a hippie approached us. He wore dirty jeans, an old cotton shirt, loose-fitting, not tucked neatly in his pants like my dad. He had long, blond hair that waved in the wind like the ropes on my dad's truck. Barefoot. He just started talking. No formal introduction such as his name, where he came from, and most importantly, why he was here in my dad's presence.

In a cool, smooth voice he said, "I can dig it, man. I can really dig it! This is how every American family should be. Living on the side of the road, doing your own thing your own way!" He nodded as he said this. My dad never looked up. He just kept hammering. The hippie continued, "you need help with that?" He was so nice. He never stopped smiling. How could he be so happy? Our lives were miserable. We were hungry, tired, and desperate. We had to get to Rhode Island because there were wealthy people there. We needed the junk they didn't want so we could sell it to buy food.

My dad was like a southern version of Archie Bunker from the 1970s show: *All in the Family*. Strangely enough, my mother was a carbon copy of Edith. They used to sing the theme song of that show; only my dad had the southern accent. My mom was every bit an Edith Bunker in her manner of speech and intellect.

Dad responded to the hippie in a low, flat tone, never looking up, "get the hell away from me." The hippie was completely unoffended, calm, and accepting. He just kept smiling, nodding, and talking. "I can dig it, man. You've been driving all day with your old lady, and you're tired. I can dig it, man. Well, if you need any help, we're just over there." He pointed to a grove of trees. I didn't see anything there. Dad never looked up. He just kept hammering. My mother had been standing next to me, but I hadn't noticed. The hippie was so intriguing. "Did he just call me 'an old lady?'" My mother asked. Dad, still hammering, smiled and replied, "yep." My mother hated hippies worse than my dad, and I think it had something to do with the 'ol' lady' statement.

After dad finished hammering, he and my brother went fishing for our supper. My sister decided to lie down in the tent. My mother and I went for a walk. Everywhere, there were beautiful and colorful wildflowers. I gathered some in a bundle. Suddenly, a bee stung me. My scream probably woke the dead and the dead-heads.

Yet again, out of nowhere, a beautiful hippie girl appeared. She must have been 18 years old but not any older. She had long blond hair with a halo of sunlight. She wore a long prairie-style cotton dress with long sleeves. She was barefoot and smiling. She leaned down—which adults never, ever did for me. She smiled, smelled of fresh flowers, and looked like an angel.

Her voice was whisper-soft. No one ever spoke so kindly to me. "What happened?" My mother responded flatly, "she was stung by a bee." The hippie chick leaned in closer to my face, and in her whisper-voice, she said, "you need aloe vera. Come with me to the van."

She took me by the hand and led me to an old, dirty white van. It was the kind that had two doors in the back. I was crying hysterically. My mother followed us. The hippie chick opened the doors. Heavy, dark-gray smoke, smelling of burnt tea, billowed out. Two hippie men were stretched out side by side like cadavers on the cargo floor of the van. They wore dirty bell-bottom jeans, long-sleeved red cotton shirts, long hair, and brown, suede Hush Puppy shoes. In a loud, scary throaty voice, the one closest to me yelled, "shut the damn van door!"

Shocked, I stopped crying. My tear froze on my cheek. I swear I heard my mother, who was standing behind me, mutter, "oh, my God." The hippie-chick was unmoved by the guy's yelling. She made her statement about my situation like a cross between a defense attorney and a paramedic. Her whisper voice was emphatic. "a little girl has been stung by a bee. She needs aloe vera."

The throaty-voiced hippie guy in the van lifted his head. The rest of his body remained completely plastered, like his consciousness, to the van floor. He looked at me through slitted eyes. I could tell I must be out-of-focus for him. The other guy never moved—a perfect cadaver.

In his throaty, strained voice, the hippie replied, "ok. But, shut the door." He exhaled audibly. More smoke billowed out. The hippie chick quickly reached up to a plant that I hadn't noticed swinging from the door frame. Another leafy plant was next to it. She was careful not to bother the leafy plant as she quickly snapped off a piece of aloe vera. She shut 'the damn van door' and leaned down to me as she had done before. "Here." She handed me a long piece of a green stick. It was slimy at the end. I fisted it. She moved my fist around my bee sting. "You're going to be ok. Just keep putting this on it." I wondered how long she could keep up in that whisper-voice. No one in my family spoke like that.

My mother nudged me. "Let's go, Carol," she ordered flatly. I think my mom thanked her, but not as nicely or as gratefully as I thought she should. I never said a word, and I hope my gratitude was known to the hippie chick who saved me. My pain was sure gone. And, now, thanks to that odd smoke, I felt very mellow. An hour after the bee incident, I kept rubbing the aloe vera on my hand. Irritated, my mother said, "you can stop that now."

My dad and brother came back from fishing. My mother told him all about the bee, the hippies, and the smoke. "Hmm." My dad replied, then asked, "do you want to move? Go to another place to camp?" My mother looked away and said, "no. Where can we go?" I didn't see any need to move. This place was paradise. My brother loved it too. We had an early supper of fried fish on a camp stove. Then, the unbelievable happened again. The first hippie guy—not the bee—came back.

He approached my dad confidently. I would have been petrified to speak to my father, but the hippie was just amused. Smiling, he said, "Hey, man. We're going to run naked and dip in the creek. So, I just wanted to let you know, because you have a family. You're welcome to join us." He said this last part while looking at my sister. My mother was horrified. My sister, all 1950s-styled with bobbed blond hair and green eyes, looked at the hippie emotionless.

My dad responded, "Oh, ok. Thanks for lettin' us know." This, the only kind response my dad gave that nice hippie who didn't have to tell us anything. My dad ordered us all in the camper like a military sergeant. We zipped it up tightly, closing all the flaps. My brother, ordered to his post in the truck, left dutifully. He may have even saluted. I don't know. No one ever disobeyed.

Dad decided that the best thing to do was to go to sleep. This was his answer for everything. If you were sick, go to sleep. Worried, go to sleep. Naked hippies you don't want to see, go to sleep!

I was not tired. A few minutes passed, and the silence broke with a holler. "Woo, Hoo!" Then, others sounding like they were running and 'woo-hooing,' joined in. Male and female voices like children playing a game of chase: feet stomping on the leaves, water splashing in all directions, laughter and happiness. I couldn't take it. I snuck out of bed and tiptoed to the front of the camper. The green canvas filled my nostrils with earthiness. Carefully I unzipped the metal zipper one notch at a time. It was hard. After all, my parents were just a foot away. Excitement filled my every fiber.

Disobedience never felt so good. I got a small part of the flap open and poked my head out of the camper. There they were: the hippies—all of them—running naked! Young men and women scurrying willy-nilly everywhere. It looked like fun.

In the background of the camper, the silence was broken by my mother's voice, "Carol. Close the tent."

CATIE BARBER

Catie Barber graduated from Richard King High School in 1996 as Catie Vasquez before moving to Austin. She homeschooled her four children until the sudden death of her 10-year-old son, Christian. For the past eight years, she's worked for *The Princeton Review* in various roles.

I Never Thought We'd End Up Here

The message said
Your daughter has been found dead
With a bag of cocaine located next to her
Please give us a call
To identify her body

My fear response has never been to
Fight or run
It has always been the absolute and abrupt
Board-stiff lack of movement
I said no
Over and over
Like a chant to bring back the dead
Or travel through time
Though the words were muddied
By dry tears
Choking my throat
As they clawed their way out
My husband stirred
Shook me
Asked what was wrong
I didn't move
I read the words over and over
White letters cast out from a green thought bubble
Such a common morning task
To check one's phone

We had no conversation of substance
For more than a year and a half
Before these letters introduced themselves
To my eyes
Sunk my heart
Into my bowels

The freeze thawed from my body
The shaking and shrieking
Took over
And I felt my husband's hands around my pregnant waist
His sobs pushing deeply into my back
I wondered silently
How I would live through this again

Her voice on the other end
A soft and scratchy
Hello
Brought my tears to the front
Poured out of my body
Straight from my heart
That was almost crushed from the reality
Of what I read
The sounds that came from my mouth
Made no sense
But the message wasn't reality
Like a police officer texting wasn't a reality

At my most vulnerable
She told me she loved me
Over and over
And apologized for some stranger's terrible prank
That felt very much like it was scripted for me
And this isn't diminished
Even slightly
By her message twelve hours later
Telling me that the phone call I made to her
Was inappropriate
And that I should not expect emotional support
From her
Because I am an adult
And it isn't her job

CHRISTOPHER ASHWORTH

Christopher Ashworth is a senior at Texas A&M University-Corpus Christi and is pursuing a Bachelor of Science in Geology. He has always enjoyed the Arts. His current artist expressions are poetry and prose.

I am not broken (a reverse poem)

I am broken
And I refuse to believe that
Someone loves me
I can see how this could be confusing, but
A broken heart can be healed
Is pure fiction
There isn't a fish for me
Once I am old and wise, I'll tell you that
I've got my own back because
Selfishness
Takes precedence over
Selflessness
Hear me out:
Once upon a time
Someone broke my heart
I remembered
Keep my head up because
My father says
Crying makes you weak
My ex says
Love comes and goes
I cannot say for certain
Love finds its way
After awhile
Hope is lost and
No longer will I sit here and act like
I know what I am doing and
It will eventually show that
I do not put forth effort
And do not assume that
I know what I am

CHARLES ETHERIDGE

A self-proclaimed desert from ElPaso, Chuck Etheridge teaches English at Texas A&M University-Corpus Christi. His poetry, fiction, and creative non-fiction have been published in a variety of reviews and books, and he has written two plays that have been produced.

Six Hundred Miles

Six hundred miles he drove
Because there weren't enough Latinos to hate in Dallas
He drove to El Paso, la frontera, my home town
To protect what he calls "America" from "invasion"

This "defender of values" pumped lead
Into a father and mother who threw their bodies across their baby to save her
Into father raising money for his daughter's soccer team
And into an elementary school teacher

This "protector" of America killed an Army staff sergeant
And a high school student
An 86 year old woman in the checkout line
And a grandfather who'd taken his granddaughter to buy her a birthday present.

Six hundred miles he drove,
And stopped at a Walmart
Because he was hungry
But changed his mind and pulled out a rifle instead of his wallet.

He drove to my hometown
Because it's where "races" mix
My beautiful mixed race son
Is a "plague" on the "purity" of his race.

He didn't know that my high school class
Had Abdous and Abouds and Esquivels and Etheridges
Sitting next to Garcias and Gilmers and Johnsons
Intermixing with Lerners and Camposes and Wallaces

600 miles he drove,
Firing at one of those classmates, who survived,

Not knowing that all of in that class—Arab, Anglo, Chinese, Latino, Black
Christian, Jewish, Muslim were all praying

For that classmate,
And for all the others who survived
And those who didn't
And for our heartbreakingly beautiful city.

He missed the point of El Paso,
That we know each other,
We like each other,
And we get along.

600 miles he drive,
Not knowing that
Even before the shooting
Those people of all races would pull together

Offering shelter, food, water,
The all of us, whatever race,
Democrat, Republican, or Partido Nacional Revolucionario
Would give money, time, hear, our prayers, anything, to help

Because mixed people,
Like metals, form alloys,
Stronger together than their component parts,
Stronger than they possibly could be if they stood alone.

600 miles he drove
To be arrested by Latino cops
To be charged by a Latino district attorney
To be arraigned by a Latino judge

I hope that, After a fair trial
They arrange to sent him
To a nice, frozen, frigid
Aztec version of hell.

Porch Prom

I call her up.
"Put on your dress and shoes."
"I can't," she says. "Prom is cancelled."
"I know. We're going to have to Social Distance."

"But I worked extra hours to buy a tux
And you and your Mom spent weeks finding that dress
And it's prom night. We're going to dress up
Even if it's cancelled."

"Let me ask my mom."
The next voice is not friendly.
"Dylan," her mom says, "I thought you had more sense.
I thought I could trust you."

"You can, Mrs. Wilson.
We'll dress up
Stay six feet apart
Stay on the front porch."

Ominous silence on the other end
"Okay," her mom says
But I'm going to keep my eye on you."
As if she wouldn't have even anyway.

I need Dad's help putting on a tux
There's this weird elastic thing
Called a "cummerbund"
And he has to tie my tie.

I use a red bandana
As a facemask,
Looking like a bandido
Taking health precautions.

Mom cries,
Takes a lot of pictures,
Says, "You look so handsome."
I shrug, embarrassed

On impulse, I go into Mom's cabinet,
Grab a Mason jar,
Fill it half full with water,
Fill the other half with wildflowers from the garden
And drive to her house.
She is standing on the porch,
My heart stops
She is more beautiful than I could have imagined

Standing in a dress of some blue-green color
Short in the front, but not too short,
Touching the ground in the back,
Shoulders bare

She looks like a princess
In those Disney movies she loves
Only she's real,
And only six feet away

Somehow, she's found a face mask
That matches her dress
And strappy heels,
Her green eyes twinkle

I ache to close the distance
But I can't
So I set the Mason jar full of flowers
On the porch

Her mother, plastic gloved,
Gives the jar the once over
With Clorox wipes
And brushes away a tear

I step to one side of the porch,
Take out on my phone
Turn on Spotify
"May I have this dance?"

Cheeks raised behind the mask,
She says, "Yes"
Going to the other side of the porch
And we dance

And we twirl
And we laugh
And I don't care
That prom was cancelled.

In my mind
We dance arm in arm
All night
Without masks.

ANTIQUE TYPEWRITER

Photo by David Lynch

Additional Keys William Mays

CHRISTIAN GARDUNO

Christian Garduno's work can be read in over 75 literary magazines. He is the recipient of the 2019 national Willie Morris Award for Southern Poetry. Garduno is a Finalist in the 2020-2021 Tennessee Williams & New Orleans Writing Contest. He lives and writes along the South Texas coast with his wonderful wife Nahemie and young son Dylan.

Monk

As I was walking to the liquor mart, I saw a monk enter the pawn shop next door. I wondered to myself if he was buying or selling. I also wondered exactly how hung-over I looked. We exited our separate stores at the same time as well, and I noticed he didn't have anything in his hands. Then it crossed my mind that they most likely low-balled him on the price of Nirvana. They hit him with the old- "Are you looking to sell or just a loan for it?". My transaction was much easier- Same thing today, pal?

Names

Looking for new stars in old cars
new chords on broken guitars
It's strange the way they give everything names
a river like Thames, a man like James
Yet no one has ever come up with a name
for that feeling I get when I see you

The Rich and The Rare

The story begins and ends in the graveyard
which I knew at the time…
I even thought about that after my first Bloody Mary
such irony at 38,000 feet above the earth….
not exactly a time to lose your marbles.....
praying to keep from looking out the window, out over the clouds, what agony
crying for mother, swearing my full name, every iota devoted to landing
clenching the armrests in gasps
Touchdown and I couldn't jump off that plane quick enough
a lay-over margarita, and I spilled it magnificently
meeting Emily by chance, sunfalling by enormous glass windows
exchanging books, numbers & looks

Holding court in a mansion, stepway to the hot tub & shower
pool table inside, fire place outside
blowing speakers and neighbors away, 91.1 FM Berkeley radio-
props, man, props
vikings and raiders
getting lost in The Old City
free BART weekend
La Val's has closed
N Judah all the way down
the Spunset, Funston, Great Expectations

And then I really put on a show
distilled unpeeled, for real
plastered sound everywhere, bouncing off the bride
the view from 17 different rooms
Radiohead live at The Bowl
Rasta Sunday night at Ashkenaz
made something out of thin air
something for us to share
Angie jamming and Kurtis on the center drum
Me banking the 7 ball
I remember Manny buckling and falling into the dresser
Felix bringing a sprinkle
Konane on the ride under the bay, explaining it to me her way
Gretchen and her sweet little friend, all energetic
Jonas and I didn't know she whined so much
she just hits that pitch

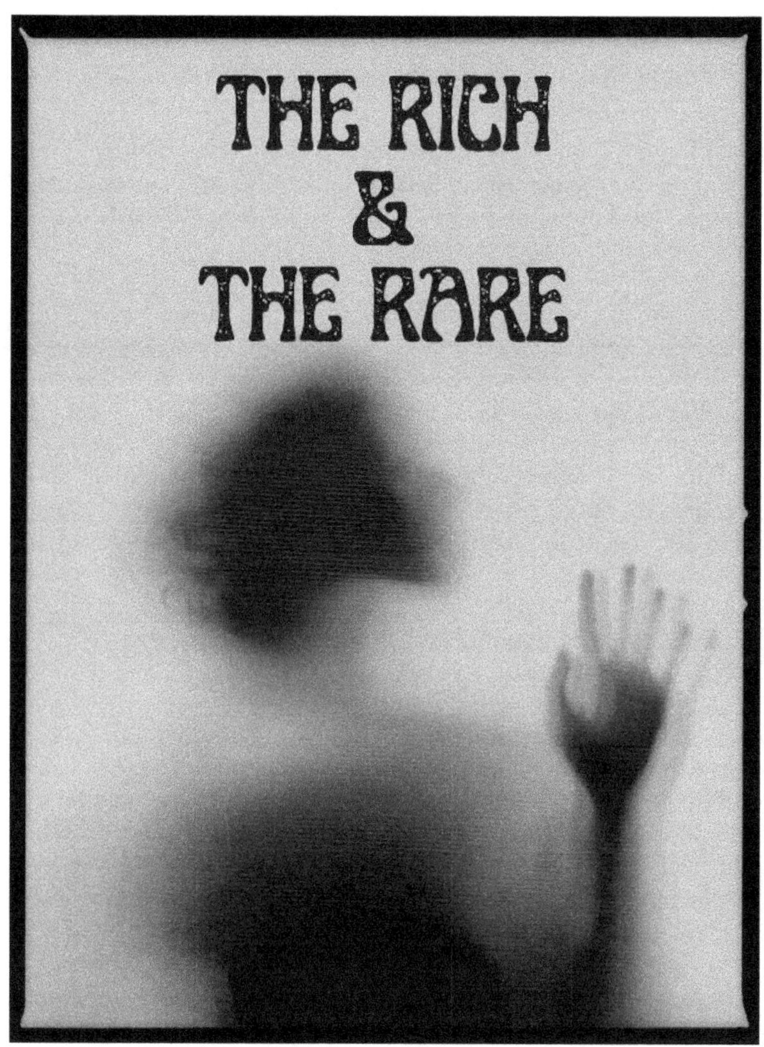

and I rubbed my hands together +
I member pouring the rum into the wine
the incense burned my fingers and swirled
I stood over the balcony and groaned
black jack all night, hit me-
hit me again.

And Honey, How Was Your Day

I sat all day on my ergonomically-correct office chair in my corner office, ignored all janitors and groundskeepers on the way to my bad-ass leased car in the parking lot, bought some gas pilfered all the way from God only knows where, and made it home by 5:45.

Time to let the wifey cook dinner from scratch, turn up the game while she checks the kiddos' homework, does all of everyone's laundry, folds it, irons it, puts it away—in between, I ask her if she can grab my charger—bathes the children, gets their day ready for tomorrow. Then, when she finally hits the couch, I have her ask me about my day. Well, really, I just Googled stuff all day, went over the Thompson account with Williams, but by then, we had to cut it short because it was lunchtime, which the company paid for, naturally. Came back to the office, talked about the game with Anderson until it was break-time, grabbed some free coffee from the break room, mentioned to Amanda in Accounting that her Pilates is certainly paying off (Mmmmm) and if she could add me on FB (the OTHER account I have on the down low).

Finally, it was time for me to shove random papers into my briefcase (I don't even know whats in there LOL). By the time I hit the elevators (entirely oblivious to the cleaning crew coming in to wash the toilets, sweep the carpeting, wipe down the elevators, toss out the stale coffee, prep the filter for the morning, etc.) I saw Jameson, and I owed him one, so I broke out the company card and we tied on a quick-double shot at Nippley's. While talking about how plump that waitress's tush is and how one day—one fine day—he's gonna ask her out and hit that, I slam my drink and I says to him- No way, man, dream on; he laughs even harder, saying: When I brutalize them cheeks, I'm gonna send you a selfie of me hitting that fo' sho'!!!

Whew, I laughed all the way across the freeway, all the way to my off-ramp, all the way down the street (where I saw some sad sap waiting for public transportation, so I splashed him), and just before I hit the corner, I slapped that garage door opener, slid the SUV right into my space, left my briefcase—I never need that damn thing—and as I turned the key into my extravagant home, I thought—Whew!! Man, that Jameson is one funny-ass dude!!!!

CRYSTAL GARCIA

Crystal Garcia is a lover of books and all things literature—especially poetry. She is the co-creator of the podcast *Revolve One* along with her brother. They seek to connect with the local community and listeners from all around the world.

My Ears Are Open

My ears are open
to listening—
yet most days
I don't want to
hear all the noises
of the world.

My ears sometimes
ring from random
electronic appliances
& spontaneous
Universal downloads.

Regardless my ears
are my own;
I do not prefer
"selective hearing"
as truth always
rings so loud and
crystal clear.

My ears will be
my own personal
recorder of what
really sticks.

These eyes
will keep watch—
however my ears
are always
actively listening.

Please watch what you say.

CYNTHIA BREEDING

Cynthia Breeding often wonders if she was born in the wrong century. She is a well-established romance writer with over 50 novels and novellas available.

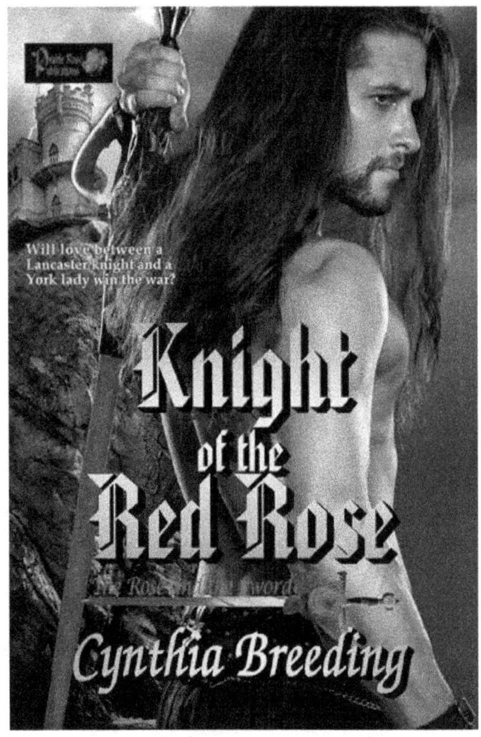

Excerpt: Knight of the Red Rose

Stephen Picard had been watching the woman with hair the color of a sunset for a few minutes before he entered the Great Hall. The clothing she wore would have attracted his attention even if the glorious cascade of red and gold curls spilling down her back like wildfire hadn't. Although the tunic and long-sleeved shirt covered most of her and the leggings and boots did the rest, it was still interesting to see a woman wearing men's clothing. Mon Dieu, it was more than that. It was intriguing. Made no less so by the fact that she carried a sword as well. Queen Margaret's spies hadn't mentioned that Edward had taken to arming females at his Court.

He glanced around to see if he could spot the king. The costumes made it difficult, but the masquerade ball had also allowed him to slip into the palace a day earlier than he was expected…all the better to get a good perspective on how things stood before he officially arrived in his capacity as emissary for King Louis on the morrow. That would involve pomp and fanfare and everyone careful to say the proper thing to establish good-will when what he needed was information about Henry, the Lancasterian king imprisoned in the Tower. Margaret, exiled in Anjou, was already planning to place her husband back on the throne with the help of the Earl of Warwick and Duke of Clarence. Stephen's real mission was to provide her—his aunt—with enough information to do it.

He felt the female warrior watching him. Mayhap he would start his quest with this one. He'd always found it easier to obtain information from women than men. Usually it was merely a matter of dropping a few compliments and acting the part of a chivalrous knight to get them talking. Besides, women often had a much more acute sense of detail than men did and battles had been lost because of a lack thereof. So, it didn't do to underestimate a woman.

He met the warrior's gaze and felt a jolt…something akin to a lightning bolt striking him. He couldn't recall ever having such a sensation before. Staring for a long moment, compulsion made him start toward her before his senses snapped him back to reality. Abruptly, he turned to melt into the crowd. He needed time to figure out why he was so drawn to her before he approached. He'd learned from his aunt to think things through and not act on impulse.

But as he circulated around the Great Hall, engaging ladies in courtly chat, he was aware that the woman dressed like a warrior queen was never far away. She didn't come close enough that he might speak to her nor did she obviously watch him as she had done when he first entered the hall. Instead, she moved unobtrusively about, almost like a zephyr wind. And yet, every fiber of his being was on high alert as though there was a potential storm brewing.

And maybe there was.

For now, he would do well to avoid the tempest and remember he was here to help restore the house of Lancaster.

CYNTHIA GIERY

Most mornings, Cynthia Giery takes her dog, Sophia, for a walk. She posts her photos and observations on Facebook

Another Gray Morning

Another gray morning spent walking under the harbor bridge. I have a fascination with the angles of this structure.

I almost skipped going over the bridge, but the fog lifted for a bit. It was so gray and misty, but still a nice walk. Then the fog rolled in again

A cold Saturday morning at Bob Hall Pier - love the blues and oranges. Sophia cutely convinced several walkers to pet her, so it's a perfect day if you're a dog.

Took a quick walk at the Corpus Christi Marina and caught a pretty bird right at sunrise. And ... there is just something about the wispy fronds on a palm that make a cool silhouette.

Driving home from our morning beach walk - where it was QUITE chilly - BB-sized hail. Neato. I guess it's winter. Took pics of the piles in my backyard. The cat was not impressed, and the dog has had enough of the cold for this morning.

Morning walk around the CC Marina. Then we went to the old Oso Pier that has been falling to pieces. Sophia was very interested in SOMETHING under the bridge, but I have no idea what it was.

It was gorgeous at the beach this morning — very little wind — so I was really enjoying the walk. Sophia ran into a big lab/Golden friend to play with, and they were romping like crazy in this cooler weather. HOWEVER, they got a little wilder than they should. Sophia rolled over and then somehow came up wrong. She was limping so our walk ended about half way. Got her into the car, home, fed and now she's resting. Pretty sure she just twisted wrong but with her back injuries I gotta be extra cautious. Sigh.
Addition: she limped out to the backyard to lay in the sun and finish her chew from yesterday.

Good morning from Bob Hall Pier. There was an odd bank of clouds surrounding the area but it was still a nice, chilly walk. I found 4 complete sand dollars and told a mom with kids where I'd put them. The kids were THRILLED when they "found" the sand dollars. It makes me happy

Merry Christmas from Bob Hall Pier — it was chilly but oh so pretty

It was FREAKING chilly this morning. The north wind was blowing so hard and the humidity made the chill waaaaay more than I planned for. However, Sophia LOVED the weather. Except when the wind blew her over TWICE while attempting to poo. I laughed because I am a horrid dog mom

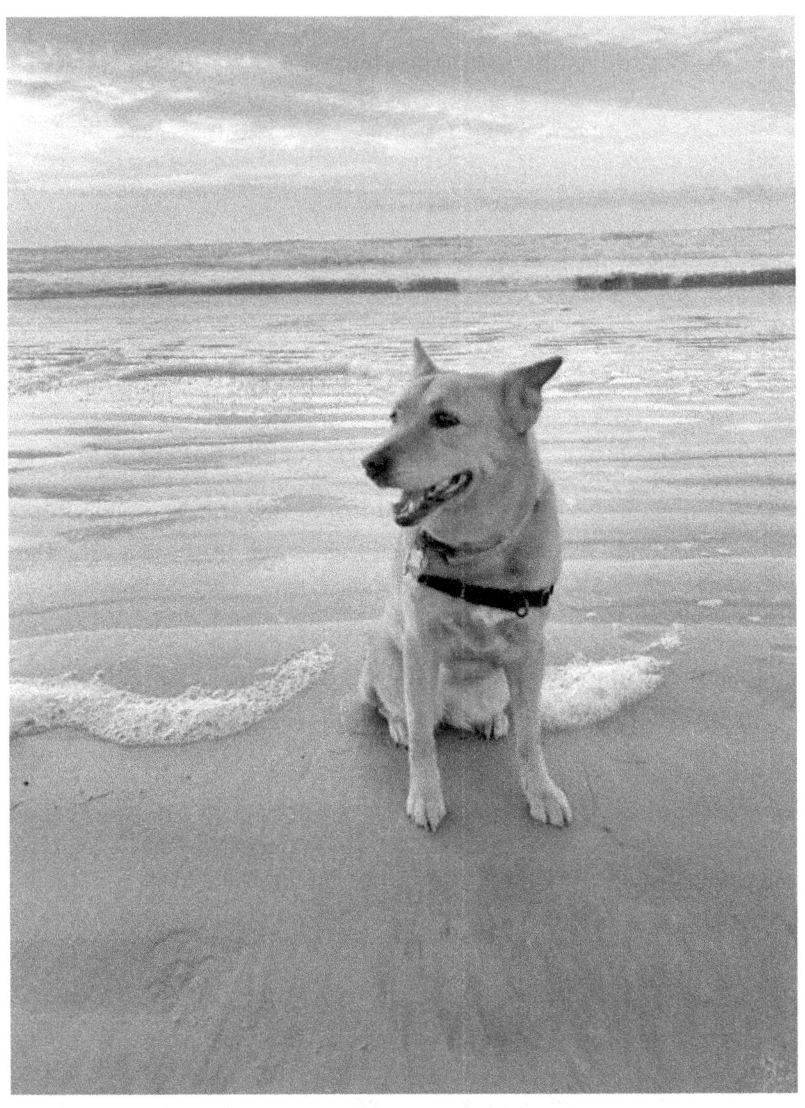

Yesterday at Whitecap Beach - it was beautiful. Possibly because I hadn't been there in so long, but it's still very pretty. Yes, I get there waaay too early, but the dawg pack has to play. Sophia chased, jumped, rolled and swam with her pack. Life is good

The weather has been incredibly beautiful this week, so, naturally, my favorite place is at the beach. Such a shame to HAVE to walk in this beauty. Sigh ...

DAVID CARPENTER

My name is David Carpenter: Writer of stories, adopter of cats, player of games. Graduate of the United States Coast Guard Academy with a second degree from the university formerly known as Corpus Christi State. After a stint in the Coast Guard, I became a computer programmer, a choice that I enjoyed but would not recommend for normal people. I live in Corpus Christi, Texas and write urban fantasy with a touch of humor.

Say the Words

It had been a bad year, a year spent hunkered down while the worst epidemic in a century cut a nasty swath through family and friends.

But I had made myself a promise, all those years ago, so here I was. Again. In a silent, wintery graveyard hundreds of miles from home, shuffling through four inches of snow to a marker I always had to look for.

You'd think I'd remember after visiting the thing 29 times.

The sky was low and gray, a jumbled mass of dark, swollen clouds that seemed to fade into a haze of tiny snow crystals that hung motionless in the air like an icy fog, reducing the grave markers to shadowy lumps of brown, gray, and white. In this light, the dim shapes all looked alike; I had to peer and squint to make out the inscriptions.

I stubbed my toe on something, causing my sciatica to flare, which sent a sharp pain shooting up my leg. I still wasn't used to it—it had been a little over a month since I hurt one of the discs in my back. I had been taking down Christmas decorations when I fell off the stepladder and twisted, trying to protect my knee, which I had hurt the week before. I blamed it on the ladder; my wife thought it was because I was starting to get old and needed to be more careful.

Like I said, it had been a bad year.

But bad year or not, I was here, limping through four inches of crunchy graveyard snow, looking for a particular marker. A small unpolished granite stone, with a simple inscription that was burned into my memory:

Jeremy Putts
Born: September 16, 1970
Died: February 25, 1991

Jeremy was a veteran, but the marker didn't mention it. His mother didn't want any references to the Army on her boy's grave. Can't say that I blame her: the Army was responsible for his death.

I know, because I was there.

He was my squad mate, but we didn't have much in common. Under normal circumstances, I would never have considered him a friend—he was a goofball with crooked teeth and a weird sense of humor. But we deployed together, so I came to know him fairly well.

His death wasn't particularly heroic. Our squad was working a mortar when something went wrong, and the round exploded in the launch tube.

Jeremy went down, riddled with shrapnel. Three or four others went down at the same time, but Jeremy caught most of it.

I was half deafened by the blast, but I did what I could—I got up off the ground, dragged him to the Humvee, and tried to stop the bleeding. I got a medal for it.

Jeremy died, and I got a medal.

Turned out I had been hit, too, but in the heat of the moment, I hadn't noticed.

I wasn't able to make it to the funeral, but I had made the trip to the cemetery every year since.

I spotted the marker and shuffled over to it, being careful not to slip and fall.

A squirrel was sitting on the gutter of a nearby mausoleum, its fluffed-up neck fur covered in a loose collar of snow, peering down on me with hard, beady black eyes.

I recognized it right away: it was my spirit guide, the totem and symbolic guardian of my clan. At least, that's what he said he was. My shrink says he's just a projection of my subconscious. He's probably right—I mean, come on, everyone knows that squirrels can't really talk. But this particular squirrel had given me some pretty good advice, so I was curious about what he was going to say this time.

I gazed up at what was probably a figment of my imagination. "You again."

"Yep. "

"Can it wait?" I nodded at the headstone. "There's something I need to do."

"I know. That's why I'm here."

"Swell."

I turned and stared down at the stone, fingering the Commendation Medal in the pocket of my jacket. I hated that medal: most of the time it resided in the big plastic box I kept in the attic. But once a year, come Hell or high water, I got it out, put it in the pocket of my jacket, and drove four and a half hours to this lonely little cemetery.

So I could stand here and remember Jeremy Putts on the anniversary of his death. I never said anything because there was nothing to say. I would just stand there, thinking about Jeremy, the explosion, and its aftermath until my feet got cold. When it reached the point where I couldn't stop shivering, I'd get back in the car, crank up the heater and drive home again.

But today was different: the squirrel was here.

And it was looking at me. I could feel those beady little eyes boring into the back of my skull.

I turned around and glared up at it. "What?"

"You gotta say the words, man."

"What the hell are you talking about?"

"Don't give me that. You know exactly what I'm talking about."

The squirrel leaped to the ground and scurried over, paws flinging bits of snow behind it.

It hopped up on the gravestone, whiskers and tail twitching, breaking the gloomy spell that the dark, sullen landscape had cast on me.

Which irritated the hell out of me. Cemeteries are supposed to be sad.

"Look at me."

I met his gaze and found myself staring into two tiny little voids of black.

"Say it." The squirrel hopped to the left side of the stone. "Go on, say it."

I looked down at the inscription and sighed. "I should have done more."

The squirrel hopped on the right side of the stone- "But?"

"But what?"

"You know what. "

I sighed again, reliving memories of my hands, slippery with blood, desperately trying to apply pressure as the light faded from his eyes.

My voice cracked a little as tears welled up.

"I did the best I could."

The squirrel hopped back to the left side and hit me with the stare again.

"Nope. Try again."

I blinked rapidly, the cold stinging my now-wet eyes. I choked a little as I said the words.

"I'm sorry you're dead. I should have done more."

It hopped back to the right, tail twitching.

"And?"

The squirrel was right—I knew what I needed to say. But it had always seemed too trivial, too trite, too inadequate to mean anything. I gazed down at the stone.

"Forgive me, brother."

The world blurred as the tears poured forth in earnest.

It was weird—until this moment, I hadn't realized just how badly I needed to say that. Jeremy had been torn up inside; the only thing that could have saved him was a full-blown medical team. A medivac was on the way, but it didn't get there in time. Intellectually, I had always known that. But I hadn't believed it. Not really.

Deep down, I had always felt guilty about Jeremy. I failed, and he died, end of story.

I pulled my hands out of my pockets, took a breath, went down on one knee, and gently placed the medal at the foot of the gravestone.

And then I straightened up, staring at what I had done. I'm not sure why, but it felt right. This is where the damn thing belonged: in a graveyard.

I wiped my eyes and heaved a heavy sigh. "Rest in peace, bro."

The tears welled up again. But then, in the middle of the hazy blur, I saw Jeremy nodding at me.

It was just for a split second: I blinked, and he was gone. When I looked up, the squirrel was gone, too.

I glanced around. I was alone, standing all by myself in the middle of a snowy field of cold, silent tombstones.

Which was reassuring, in an odd kind of way.

I took one last look at the inscription. I didn't need to see this anymore: I was never going to forget Jeremy. I would carry the memory of that gap-toothed goofball until I was laid into a grave of my own.

I squared my shoulders, turned around, and started limping back to my car.

My feet weren't cold yet, but I had done what I came here to do. It was time to move on.

DEVORAH FOX

"What if?" Those two words all too easily send Devorah Fox spinning into flights of fancy. She writes mysteries, fantasies, and thrillers, and is the author of 50 books and short stories.

Title Illustration by Kayla Matt

Excerpt from *The Demon of Corpus Christi*

If I failed to submit my story on time, I'd never get a chance like this again. The deadline loomed, but I couldn't be more firmly stymied if I were cast in quick-drying cement. I couldn't squeeze out another syllable if my life depended on it. My life didn't, but the opportunity sure did. I'd accepted an invitation to contribute to an anthology. My first publication credit! My writing career would only go up from here. I was nearly done but needed a killer ending, something to resonate with readers. The closing date for submissions hanging over my shoulder cast a shadow on my keyboard. I felt the deadline's hot breath on the back of my neck.

I fired up my work playlist, jazz instrumentals that I find relaxing and freeing, but I did more chair-dancing than writing. I left my living room writing niche and fixed my favorite coffee. The legend on the mug mocked me—Writer's Block: When Your Imaginary Friends Won't Talk To You. I tried all my trusty block-breaking tricks to no avail.

Ernest Hemingway once said, "In order to write about life, first you must live it."

He might be right. I should step away from this desk, go experience something.

A drive. I'd take a short excursion away from the city. A long blank stretch of blacktop without traffic to contend with would allow my thoughts to wander. I'd stop trying to force the words to come and would instead open my mind, take inspiration from my surroundings.

Making sure that I had a pen in my purse, I grabbed a bottle of water. I got into my little Kia Soul crossover. When I leaned over to stash my water in the cup holder, the edge of my bag hit a button, which activated the navigation system.

"Enter your destination," prompted a disembodied woman's voice.

Yikes, the car was talking to me! I had, at times, talked to the car and in admittedly harsh terms, but this was creepy.

I didn't have a ready answer. Where to go? I glanced at the electronic display for the navigation option, a feature I never use. I rarely go anywhere unfamiliar.

"Enter your destination," the voice repeated.

I felt on the spot, like being called on by the teacher when I hadn't done my homework. Frantic, I scoured the display prompts for help. Home? No, I was already home. Street Address? No, I had none to supply. Points of Interest?

Okay, now we were talking, no pun intended. I selected that and received Nearby Restaurants, Nearby Gas Stations, Nearby ATMs. None of those were what I had in mind. The Search By Category option looked promising. I chose it and scrolled through the selections until I found

Tourist Attractions. I had been to most of them, but one was new to me: the Selena Museum. I had seen her memorial statue on Corpus Christi's bayfront but a museum? What could be in it? How big could it be? It might be the ticket for a quick jaunt. Then revitalized, recharged, back to work.

Another choice caught my eye: the Demon of Corpus Christi.

Say what? I chuckled. I guess I had heard something about that: a huge fiberglass construction, once part of an amusement park ride that was salvaged by a scrap metal business.

Oh, why not? I said to myself, but not to the GPS lady because who knew where that would send me? I selected the Demon of Corpus Christi and backed down the driveway.

"Head southeast for 358 feet," the lady said.

Before I figured out how far that was, the lady told me to take a "slight right toward Ennis Joslin Road, for one-tenth of a mile" followed by "slight right onto Ennis Joslin Road, eight-tenths of a mile. Turn right onto Nile Drive. Get on Texas 358 West, eight minutes, two-point three miles."

Why didn't you just say, "Get on SPID?" I wanted to ask but didn't for fear of what response that would provoke. I headed for the familiar freeway.

"Turn right onto South Padre Island Drive," my electronic copilot said.

See? Why didn't you say that in the first place? I retorted silently.

Further instructions directed me toward the Leopard Street exit. An industrial area, it houses recycling centers, spare car-parts lots, an asphalt plant, a metal fabricator.

I jounced over a stretch of road where the expansion joints sounded like horses clomping. "Sorry," I said to the GPS lady. The audio for the navigation system crackled, and for a moment was a flurry of static. "Recalculating," came a garbled voice.

Was there a problem with the system? Had I jarred something loose, annoyed my navigator? What if she deserted me? I didn't know the exact location of the Demon of Corpus Christi. I supposed that if I couldn't find it, I could simply turn around and go home. After all, I did get a little drive. Maybe I would be ready to get back to work.

The navigation system crackled again. "Recalculating. Exit onto Mckinzie Road," said a new voice, this time a male. I knew the system offered a variety of narrator personalities. Perhaps the interruption to the signal had made a new selection. I could restore the female voice if I dared to fiddle with the controls. But this voice was intriguing: clear, authoritative, with a hint of seductive charm, like a voice-over artist for a TV commercial.

I followed the instructions, although the further I drove, the less populated the area became. I passed a concrete plant, a distribution warehouse, and a nursery. Then structures of any kind became fewer and farther between. I drove past a lot of open country, the scrubby foliage crisping in the summer sun. It made me thirsty and glad I had brought water.

I drove for miles, keeping to the route to which I had been directed. Finally, I decided that not only was I not nearing the Demon of Corpus Christi but also I was lost.

—END of EXCERPT—

"The Demon of Corpus Christi" by Devorah Fox continues in *Unknown Realms: A Fiction-Atlas Press Anthology* by C.L. Cannon, https://books2read.com/b/unknownrealms.

Excerpted with permission.

DONNA HUDDLESTON

Before her retirement, Dr. Donna Huddleston served at Del Mar College as a nurse educator in the Department of Nursing Education. Currently, she is the Lead Nurse Planner at Del Mar College, Department of Continuing Education. A graduate of Purdue University and the University of Illinois (UIC) at Chicago, where she earned her Ph.D., she has a long history of service to the community as a public health nurse and home health and hospice administrator. She has numerous publications and presentations, including international research works.

When the Door Opened

When the front door opened, the wind rushed in, blowing the pages in my book. My husband, Lee, swept in with the wind—and collapsed in a heap on the foyer floor.

"Donna, help me," he said.

As a nurse, I pride myself on knowing what to do in these situations. My first thought was a heart attack known as myocardial infarction, and the second thought was a stroke.

"Do you have chest pains?" I asked as I dialed 911.

He was not exhibiting signs of a stroke—he could speak and move both his arms and both of his legs. He was not unconscious, but his skin was blue. He was going into shock, and I wrapped my blanket around him to keep him warm.

My husband—tall and slim with no risk factors for a heart attack—could die.

"The ambulance is coming," I told him. "Don't worry."

Hopefully, he could not see the anxiety I felt. Him staying calm was imperative. The seconds ticked by and felt like hours. Finally, the siren approached, and I ran out to the yard.

"Hurry," I begged.

They wouldn't let me in the ambulance, so I hugged their bumper and pulled into the ER right next to him. Like a wilted flower, the oxygen and intravenous fluids he had received in the ambulance had perked him up. The ER staff whisked him away for various tests, including an endoscopy where they viewed inside his stomach. I waited in an emergency room bay.

A physician told me lab tests revealed he had lost most of his blood. How did that happen? There had been no visible signs of bleeding but causes jumped wildly through my mind. Did he hurt himself outside? No. Had he been shot? Did someone stab him? Even the thoughts of a vampire flickered across my mind. I was beside myself. How did he lose all his blood?

Treatment was straightforward: Lee needed a blood transfusion. He was O positive. The hospital did not have any, and a delay of even a few minutes would be life-threatening. Our adult son was O positive. We had left messages but were unable to reach him.

My husband's life seemed about to slip away when our son raced in, a panicked expression on his face. We explained what we knew as the phlebotomist hurriedly drew his blood for a type and cross-match. Perfect. Within the next hour, James, our son, donated two pints of blood. The blood was still warm as it infused into Lee's veins. Soon, the blueness left, and Lee was more like his old self.

A few hours later, Lee was sitting up in the hospital bed when a surgeon entered. "I'm Dr. Charles," he said. The physician looked young with a full head of dark hair and a white, unbuttoned lab coat. He sat down on a chair at the end of the bed and started talking. I was ready to hear the worst, but he asked mundane questions. Where did we live? What did we do for a living? How many grandchildren did we have?

As a nurse, we know that most doctors are in and out of patient rooms. I squirmed in my chair, wanting a diagnosis before he went to the next patient.

"He has an ulcer in his stomach," he finally said to me. "Most patients, if they are still bleeding, will be up going to the bathroom multiple times. I don't see this with you," he said to Lee. "I believe, when you collapsed at home, shock clamped the stomach ulcer we saw on the tests. It's not bleeding now. From your tests, we know a bacteria, Helicobacter pylori, caused it."

H. pylori bacteria invade the stomach lining, and in most people, it's not harmful. For my husband, it created a bleeding ulcer. He had ignored the warning sign of tarry, black stools for several days before his collapse. Dr. Charles prescribed an antibiotic, Flagyl (metronidazole). It eradicated the H. pylori, and his bleeding ulcer did not return.

Why did it attack my husband? H. pylori is an opportunistic organism found in the gastrointestinal tract of up to fifty percent of the population. It lies dormant until something triggers it to invade the stomach lining. With Lee, the bacteria, after digging around inside his stomach, found a blood vessel.

The fates were kind to us. Lee fully recovered from his bout with H. pylori. He did not have any more episodes of gastrointestinal bleeding. On most Sundays, we reflect on our lived experiences. We are both grateful for the knowledgeable care he received.

DONNA LEA ANDERSON

Donna Lea Anderson's second novel is actually three children's novels in one. It tells the stories of Hummie, Sammie, and Attie.

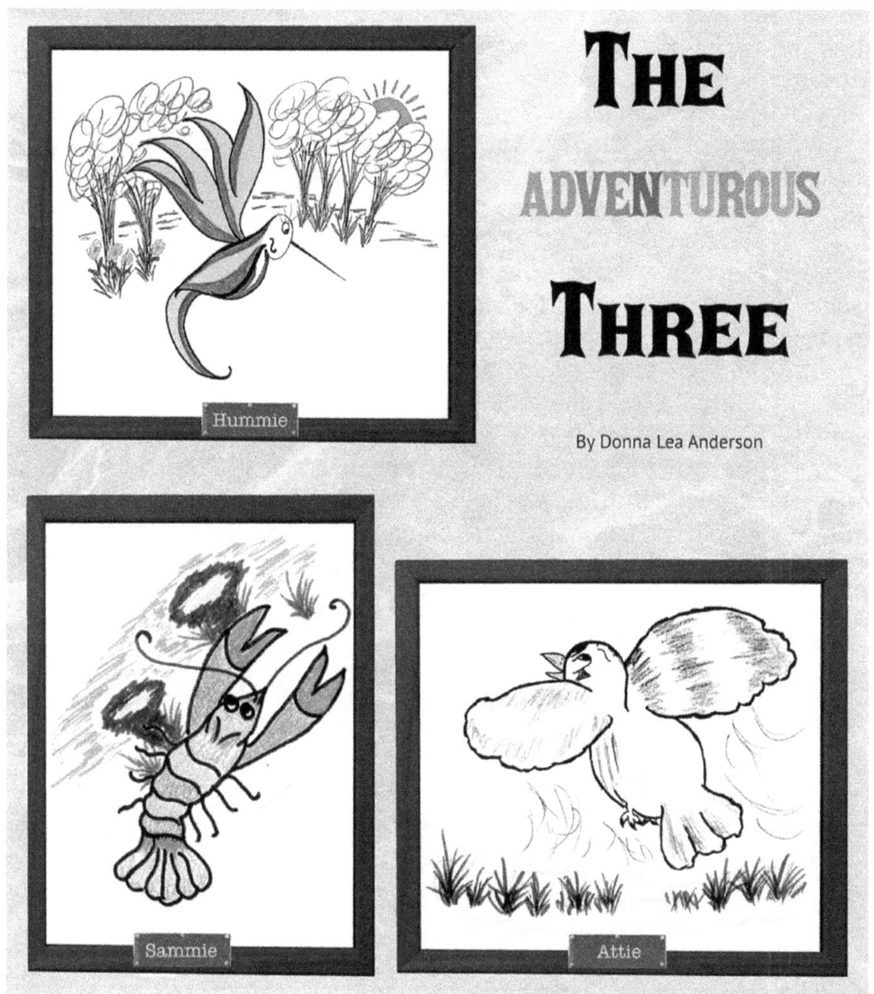

Excerpt from *Saving Hummie*

When the garage doors open, they find the tiny hummingbird still sitting on the wire where they last saw him. It looks like his eyes are closed, and for some reason, his head is slumped over. He is not swarming about fluttering his bright yellow and green wings!

McKenna whispers because she thinks he is asleep, but Grandpa has his doubts and worries about him. He has her keep a close eye on him while he sets up for his garage project.

Twenty minutes pass; Grandpa notices that the bird has not even moved an inch. He decides that it is time to get a tall ladder, climb up, and get a closer look at him. Trying not to scare his little ballerina, he gets her involved. Her job is to help carry the ladder and then hold it while Grandpa climbs up to check.

With McKenna watching from below, Grandpa finally reaches the top of the ladder and moves very carefully, trying not to spook the little guy. Once he sees the severe condition of the hummingbird, he mumbles under his breath, "Aw, little guy, you're so much worse than I anticipated."

McKenna calls out, "What's wrong, Grandpa?"

"Bad news, sweet girl. It looks like he is sick. Please hold the ladder steady, and I'll bring him down so we can give him some medicine."

McKenna says, "Ok, Grandpa, I'll hold the ladder."

Gently, he cups the little guy into the palm of his hand and begins to make his way down. Once he has both feet on the ground, he squats down in front of McKenna. This is the first time she has ever seen a hummingbird up close, and she is in awe. She can't believe how small the little guy is. She watches closely as Grandpa attempts to get him to move.

Sadly, his little body remains limp. Grandpa even tries to hold his little head up, but it continues to slump back over to one side. He is not doing good at all and needs help immediately.

McKenna says, "He is really sick, isn't he, Grandpa?"

Grandpa replies, "He sure is my sweet granddaughter. It seems he exhausted himself yesterday and during the night trying to get out of the garage."

When McKenna begins to tear up, Grandpa tells her that he believes that the little guy needs medicine which is nothing more than nourishment. He has her sit on the concrete floor and stick her index finger out. Soon the little hummingbird is perched on her finger and holds on for dear life!

Excerpt from *Crawfish Sammie.*

Once upon a time, there was a little mudbug named "Crawfish Sammie." He lived in Gonzales, Louisiana, near a lily pad pond surrounded by beautiful, luxurious homes on a golf course.

What is a mudbug? Some folks claim mudbugs are crayfishes, often referred to as crawfish or crawdads.

Crawfish Sammie is a colorful crawfish; he resembles a miniature lobster. He is a shellfish with two tiny red claws, two tiny dark eyes, and two long antennae poking out from atop of his itsy-bitsy head.

He doesn't live in a house like you and me. He lives in a three-foot burrow underground—which he built all by himself! What is a burrow?

A crawfish burrow has a cone-shaped mound. It's called a "chimney," and it stands about eight inches above the ground. It's the only way in and out of the burrow.

Excerpt from *Independent Attie*

"Fearless Attie" wants to learn more about her surroundings even though she is still unable to fly. "No time for breakfast," she tells her siblings. "I want to see the world."

Convinced that seeing the world and all of its glory is fun and exciting, she takes an early morning stroll, waddling through the grass and sticking close to the fence. Playfully, she skips and hops as she goes—until she spots Mimi.

She takes off running. Pretty much flying at times. Yep, she sprints across the grass and that's when she screams out to the world and her family on how she really feels. She is busted by Mimi, the Backyard Landlady!

DYLAN LOPEZ

Dylan Lopez is a junior at Texas A&M University-Corpus Christi pursuing a degree in English. A student of Joseph Wilson and Tom Murphy, he is currently the Assistant Managing Editor for The Windward Review.

Reveries from Orbit

A muddled stain of lights struggles past
nebulous pillars, primordial constants
drifting across a stellar stage—
endlessly expanding.

Far expelled from the hunting grounds of Arcadia,
shamed Callisto rolls through her endless night—
like a battered pearl embracing magnetic tempests,
bound to a vicious, lunar circuit.

Cold is the gardener's land without those tender stars,
beaming flares born in the dust-filled, knotted veils
of Chaos, noble pyres spend to the embers,
furnishing fields and skies with humble glow.

And I, on my cosmic dérive aboard a Catherine wheel,
break from the stellar tides, parsing through wondrous
trails of light and muted fields of slumbering stones,
out into the vast astral scenery, to find myself.

There's no such thing as more than friends

There's no such thing as more than friends
For coupled hearts severed, with green wounds;
This bitter feeling, on you depends

Though we have tried late to make amends
For mercy well-hidden, cannot be found;
There's no such thing as more than friends

This lasting indifference, to you extends
A craving verse, sung without a sound;
This bitter feeling, on you depends

A loading thought from your phone sends
this carousel of broken dreams around;
There's no such thing as more than friends

All at once, your carny fantasy ends
To that tempting dream, I was bound;
This broken feeling, on you depends

A snuffed ember that we couldn't tend,
Polaroid ashes, scattered on the ground
There's no such thing as more than friends
This broken feeling, on you depends

Torch Singer

Carved into a wrinkled cerebral alleyway,
there sits a lounge styled in gentle noire.
Deserted halls of spent cigarettes and
lip-touched bottles bend at the wistful
song of a velvet chanteuse on the stage.

She plies her trade on live, neural wires—
neurons firing on her siren-sung notes that
that hang on yesterday's seductive hopes.
It's the last call of someone's love omitted,
held in a languid space between the eyes.

In her last refrain, she takes from the stage
down into rows of empty velvet seats and
sunken lights bright with her intensity.
Like a flickering bulb, she sparks against
a heavy node, crooning down the axons:

Will you remember me,
As I remember you?

ESTHER BONILLA READ

Esther Bonilla Read was born and raised in Calvert, Texas, a small town in Central Texas. She graduated from Baylor University and began teaching school in Corpus Christi, Texas. She has been published by various newspapers, *Chicken Soup for the Latino Soul,* and several anthologies and magazines.

My Mother Finally Speaks Up

Mother and Daddy came from Mexico, and after they met and married, followed the Mexican protocol in raising their families. My father was the head of the family and made all decisions relating to home and family, and Mother seemed quite happy with the arrangement. In fact, in school when a teacher said, "I'll speak to your mother about it." I always wondered why she didn't say, "I'll speak to your father about it."

In addition to the obvious cultural differences Mother and Daddy practiced, there were other differences they must have noticed, such as the lack of ingredients necessary to make Mexican food. There were no avocados at the stores, no large peppers, no corn tortillas, and no masa needed to make corn tortillas or tamales. In Calvert, our hometown located in central Texas, no remnants of the culture they left behind were to be found.

I had noticed an odd thing on our back porch for some time that someone had given us or abandoned on our back porch. It was a rectangular stone that sat slanted toward the two short legs in front. A taller leg in the back completed it. A separate oblong-shaped stone lay on top it, all made of speckled stone. Lava stone, someone explained to me.

Mother said it was a metate (may-tah-tay) an antique used in Mexico and other countries in central and South America to grind corn, a staple eaten in all of the Americas. A "mano" was another part of the process used to grind corn. It was the oblong object you pushed to do the job. You would mash the corn, and a receptacle sat near the two legs to catch the ground-up corn. The metate was never used by anyone. It sat all alone on the back porch year after year, suffering the anger of the wind, rain, and snow. The fig tree lost leaves and found themselves nestled in the metate, that is until the rain came and bathed it and waited for the sun to dry it out.

My father, who operated a service station seven days a week, knew everyone in town. In addition, his place of business was a sort of way station. People would stop and sell him fish, eggs, vegetables, apples, oranges, or whatever they had to sell. If he found a good deal, he brought it to our home, which was full of boisterous children.

Mamá Grande or Grandmother, who lived in a small town in south Texas, came to visit us in Calvert about once a year in the summer. She had deep wrinkles on her face and wore dresses down to her ankles, and she put up with nothing from us. She sewed beautifully and made the girls nice dresses. Mother was delighted to have her mother visiting us. We had to admit having her around was a very good thing.

Daddy walked in one day with a grocery bag full of fresh corn, exclaiming, "Look what I've got!" Mother was happy, and we thought we would eat corn on the cob with butter I churned made from the cream from our cow. It was all a happy scene.

At that very moment, I think the cosmos conspired by bringing together my grandmother, the corn, and the metate. How else could the following have occurred?

Grandmother put her hands on her hips and, looking at my father, said, "Ruben, I can make tortillas de maíz (corn tortillas) with that corn, and I'll use the metate.

The next morning Grandmother arose and, wearing an apron over her long dress, prepared everything she would need to convert the corn to masa. She had prepared the kernels and then washed and cleaned the metate and the mano. All in all, she was ready for the task. I stood to the side, ready to run any errand she might need.

She set up the metate on the porch and placed a shallow bowl at the front of the metate. Meanwhile, she kept a large bowl with the prepared corn near her. She placed a folded towel on the porch, sat on her knees, and began the grinding process. Pressing down and pushing. Pressing and pushing. After a while, she had an ample supply of ground-up corn or corn masa (dough).

She brought in the masa and placed a griddle on the stove to heat. She made balls out of the corn dough and then moved the individual balls from hand to hand in a slapping motion until she had a fat corn tortilla, something we had never seen in central Texas. She placed one on the hot greased griddle and, after a few seconds, flipped it over with a spatula. She continued until she had a nice stack of hot, homemade, thick tortillas de maíz on a plate. The smell of the toasted tortillas caused my mouth to water.

Meanwhile, Mother prepared lunch and placed the homemade salsa in the molcajete (like a mortar and a pestle) in the middle of the table beside the vermicelli and ground beef bowl. Daddy came in, took a whiff of the aroma, and smiled. All of us sat at the table and enjoyed a most unusual meal. Daddy said to her mother-in-law, "Mamá, these tortillas are wonderful!" And looking toward my mother, added, "I hope María will make these when you leave."

My mother, all four feet-eleven-inches tall, stood up and exclaimed, "I shall never do that!" We turned to look at Daddy, who laughed it off, perhaps just to save face. And that is how we learned that Mother could stand up for herself. And Mother never did get down on her knees to grind corn. She only got on her knees to pray when we went to church.

West Texas
By Gerald Beckman

GERALD BECKMAN

Gerald Beckman was born and raised on a farm in West Texas and practiced law in Corpus Christi for many years. Since retirement, he has written several novels. These include *The Family, When Latin Lost Its Relevance, Roughnecks and Rednecks*, and *Powder Road.* His work is intensely evocative of all things Texas—whether it's West Texas or South Texas. Recently, he's taken up oil painting, often choosing the rugged, West Texas terrain as a subject.

A Cold Day in Hell

Cecil parked his pickup beside his office. A strong north wind had blown in during the night – not all that unusual this time of year, except this one carried snow with it.

The snow wouldn't amount to much, though. This kind of wind would sweep the fields and plains clean of snow no matter how much fell, piling it into drifts with fantastic shapes along fence rows and bar ditches and on the lee sides of buildings. None of it would add any moisture to the drought-stricken fields or pastures in this part of the Texas Panhandle.

Well, let it blow. Neither drought nor blizzard slowed his practice down any. Legal problems proliferated in good times and bad, and that's why he was in the office when the weather would have been a good excuse not to be. A problem solver is what he was. He rejected some folks' notion that he made a living off the sufferings of other people, though there might be a kernel of truth in the contention.

He hung up his coat and checked his calendar. The deposition of an expert witness at ten, a docket control conference at two.

He glanced at the street outside his window. The swirling flurries seemed to be coming straight from the arctic ice cap.

He checked the call slips Rosie had stuck on his spindle. Standard stuff. A realtor, an adjuster, a court reporter – he'd return them after the two o'clock conference. He'd need to spend the morning preparing to depose the defendant's expert.

He liked deposing experts. He had a knack for finding the nugget in a witness's testimony and felt like he could do it in his sleep, but he didn't want to take a chance on this one. Most of his injury cases were small potatoes, but this one involved the death of a young father of four. It would mean a huge payday if the expert testified as expected on cross.

He had just begun reviewing his notes when the intercom buzzed.

"Better take line three," Rosie said. "He won't identify himself but says he won't call again."

She had perfect pitch when it came to deciding which calls demanded immediate attention. He lifted the receiver.

"Ain't none of my business," the caller said without preamble, "but I drive by your pasture every day, and I been noticing your cows crowding the fence bawling like they're starving to death. Ain't Otto supposed to be taking care of 'em?"

Otto was a fifty-year-old bachelor who earned minimum wages doing odd jobs for local farmers and ranchers. He worked hard when he worked but never let ambition get in the way of hunting geese or fishing for crappie in Buffalo Lake.

"Yes, as a matter of fact…"

"Well then, I guess you ain't heard. The damn fool stumbled chasing after a downed goose, and his gun went off.. Shot three toes off his left foot. He ain't been out of his house for nearly a week."

A week? His cows hadn't been fed for a week? Ah, Christ…

"Damn, I hate to hear that. Hope he's okay. Know anybody willing to carry a pickup load of hay out there right now, this morning, maybe check the windmill? I'd be glad to pay whatever it takes."

"I don't know anybody like that, and it ain't my call to find one."

"Well…"

"Those damn cows need attention. If you can't do it, you best get out of the business."

The caller hung up.

Cecil had spent his whole professional life standing up to intensely practical people who didn't hesitate voicing aversion to his charging a hundred dollars an hour for examining leases and attending water district meetings, or a minimum of a thousand dollars defending a DWI charge. Even less was he inclined to defer to them in a matter of personal conduct. Yet this coarse, angry voice had stirred a flush of shame.

Now what? He didn't know anybody willing to face a blizzard to save the hide of an absentee land owner who didn't have sense enough to take care of his own cows. He knew the opinion many farmers had of arrogant doctors and lawyers who bought up all the land they could get their hands on, then flaunted their ownership like an English Lord while paying bottom wages to misfits to do the dirty work, rather than leasing it out to self-respecting farmers like themselves. The caller was undoubtedly one of them.

What could he have been thinking, buying a 640-acre patch of dry caliche pasture with barely enough ground water to feed a windmill, and steep bluffs dropping a hundred feet all along the south half?

The idea had been to buy a few acres, hold them till he got tired of practicing law, then sell the whole shebang and hope to make enough to retire on. But the land was worth less now than when he bought it ten years ago. So why not make a few bucks raising cows? Hire somebody like Otto to haul them a load of hay every other day and count them, check the windmill and make sure the fence stayed in good repair – it would be easy…

It might have been a crank call, but since Otto didn't have a phone, Cecil couldn't verify the story. He'd have to run out to check on his cows personally. Thirty minutes to the pasture, thirty back. If they really were short of feed, it wouldn't take more than a day or two to find someone to take Otto's place. The cows could get by on the scant pickings that long.

He put his coat back on and hurried out the door, assuring Rosie he'd be back in time for the deposition.

The wind nearly jerked the door out of his hands.

His pasture was four miles south of the community of Bright, and Bright, sometimes still referred to by its German name Hell by people who saw the humor in it, was fifteen miles west of his office.

The wind picked up on the way, buffeting his pickup and sending the snow flying horizontally. Visibility was down to a quarter-mile, and the temperature couldn't be over twenty. Tumbleweeds blew across the highway like they were fleeing in terror. He pulled on his driving gloves and shivered.

Thirty head of cattle. Three hundred dollars a head, tops, probably not that given the shape they would be in if they hadn't been fed properly. Nine thousand dollars at most if they were all still alive, and the deposition was part of a case that would bring ten, maybe twenty times that, just for his fee. So why was he wasting time on a miserable bunch of cows? If he had any sense, he'd turn his pickup around and get his ass back to the office.

Instead, he turned off the highway onto the section road running by his pasture.

What he saw nauseated him. The animals were skin and bones, heads hanging, necks scarred and bleeding from pushing their heads through the barb wire fence reaching for dry weeds; listless, facing downwind, visibly shivering. Clearly they had been hungry for longer than a week. He had assumed that even if the call were genuine, it would be an exaggeration. The cows had 640 acres, after all, and there were only thirty of them. Surely they could find enough pickings between the caliche rocks and prickly pear to survive on, but they looked like so many sacks of rattling bones.

He called his office from his cell phone.

"I can't make the deposition," he told Rosie, "and I can't get hold of Joe. Call him for me, will you? Tell him…tell him I have to feed my cows."

He detected disbelief in her silence.

"I have to have more than that," she said. "His expert is driving in from Tulsa – he's probably already here – and you know what a jerk Joe can be. He'll go for sanctions, and with Judge Harlan he might get them."

"Well then, don't call him. If I'm not there when he and his witness show up, tell him…tell him you don't know where I am, but I'll make it as soon as I can."

Yeah, opposing counsel didn't owe him any favors, and Joe was the type who believed his duty to his client obliged him to take every advantage. And Judge Harlan – Cecil wished he had never gotten involved in that particular campaign. Harlan was a vindictive son-of-a-bitch with a long memory. Cecil had already tasted the bitter fruits of choosing the wrong side of that race, and Harlan wouldn't let a few hungry cows get in the way of his idea of justice, especially if their condition was the result of Cecil's own neglect, which Joe would be sure to point out. Joe might even argue it was a case of cruelty to animals, and he might be right. How much of a defense would trusting a guy like Otto amount to?

All of which was beside the point. These poor animals were suffering the pains of the damned, and his only choice was to get them feed immediately. He'd have to take his chances with Joe.

He had been buying hay from Edwin Wilke, a shrewd old farmer who had bought up all the wheat straw he could get his hands on for nearly nothing, then baled it for resale to cattlemen he knew would be in desperate need long before the drought ended. His farm was five miles north of Bright, but when Cecil got there, Edwin had taken a load of hogs to market, so Cecil had to load the twenty bales himself.

Suit, tie, overcoat, low-top shoes, thin socks, and driving gloves of fine Italian leather – hardly the garb for loading hay. Thirty years since he had lifted a bale, but the feeling of the taut wire under his gloved fingers was as fresh as the wind in his face.

The load shifted on the way to the pasture, making it too unsteady to stand on when unloading in the pasture. He had to pull the bales off the tail end of the pickup from the ground while the hunger-crazed animals pushed and shoved against him, smearing their freezing and dripping snouts on his clothes. Then he had to jostle the animals to retrieve the wires so they wouldn't get tangled in their hooves.

He extricated his pickup from the melee and drove to the windmill fifty yards from where he dumped the bales. Six inches of ice had formed on the water in the stock tank. After thirty frustrating minutes of chopping with his lug wrench and producing a hole the size of a dinner plate, he thought to turn on the windmill. The wheel spun for five long minutes before water finally began pouring out of the discharge pipe to spread across the ice, hopefully faster than it would freeze.

By now, a thin line of cows was trotting clumsily toward the water, heads low, jerking from side to side, slinging saliva as they came. It broke his heart to see them.

The day began to clear, but the wind, strong as ever, continued pushing wispy clouds across the sky. It forced bitter cold through his ruined clothes and tattered gloves, but he continued facing into it, numb, shivering, and dejected by what awaited him at the office. By now, Joe would have produced his witness, made his record, and dictated a motion for sanctions. What defense could Cecil muster against a hostile opponent and a judge nursing a grudge?

He thought he remembered Rosie paying his E&O premium but felt a sudden need to be certain. With frozen fingers, he punched autodial on his cell phone. He turned away from the wind so he could hear Rosie's voice.

"Rosie..."

"I've been trying to call you," she said, "Joe called."

Oh shit, here it comes. "I figured. What'd he say?"

"He wants to reschedule."

"Reschedule? What does he want to reschedule?"

"The deposition. The blizzard has closed Interstate 40 from Amarillo to Shamrock, and his expert can't make it through."

"What did you tell him?"

"Said I'd have to clear it with you."

Suddenly the frigid air changed from bitter and biting, to clean, fresh, and friendly. He breathed it deep, savoring it. His gaze lingered out over the barren breaks and the range country beyond. It all now looked wild and free and oh, so lovely.

"You still there?" Rosie said. "This connection isn't so good..."

"Yeah, yeah I'm still here. Tell him we can reschedule, but he'll owe me one — no, don't tell him that. Just...just reschedule the damn thing."

Why tempt fate on such a gorgeous day?

HEATHER TWARDOWSKI

R.C. Seiner, aka Heather Twardowski, holds a B.A and M.A in English from Texas A&M University-Corpus Christi. Currently, she serves as an Instructional Consultant at the Stone Writing Center and an adjunct for the English department at Del Mar College. She loves dystopian fiction as well as sci-fi, mystery, and supernatural.

Excerpt from *Outcast Island*

If you asked the young Will Powers where he thought his life would go, never would he imagine himself in an old, ritzy estate in the center of Scotland. Or himself incarcerated in an old, ritzy estate in the center of Scotland. Or himself incarcerated in an old, ritzy estate in the center of Scotland, forced to solve murder cases with an ex-art thief, an ex-Mob boss, an ex-terrorist, and ex-murderer.

Nope. He would not think that in the slightest.

As it begins, Will had a run-in with a bit of legal trouble back in his home of Stonehaven. Without going too much into detail this early in the story, Will had faced several accusations of causing a woman to disappear, as he possessed the slightly undesirable trait of sociopathy.

A sociopath with a fascination of death, murderers, and murder tactics.

Although the two remain unrelated.

But because of the poor, paranoid nature of humans, Will faced the choice of spending up to five years in prison while the investigation continued, or he could confess, regardless of if he did it or not. An unfair choice, really, but thankfully he didn't need to choose.

The story begins on the gloomy day of Will's trial. The townspeople flocked to witness the fate of Stonehaven's Most Wanted. Will stood stoically before the judge and lazily counted the amount of times the justice blinked. Or composed a rhythm from the fidgeting fingers of the jurors against the dark oak benches. His eyes would peer at those who coughed or gritted their teeth, making quite a few shift uncomfortably in their seats as he set his sights on them. Every so often, a "witness" would come up to the stands and speak a few nonsensical words about how they saw Will lurk around a cemetery or accuse him of occult practices.

The accusations had no real effect on Will anymore. On the contrary, he didn't care. Of course, he couldn't feel anything anyways. Although, he found it amusing that the townspeople still put him at the top of the list whenever some uncommon crime occurred in the small city. At this point, Will only desired that his accusers would come up with better stories, other than the same old suspicions. He had hoped that maybe this trial would possess something different.

You can imagine Will's surprise when the tall, lanky man in the black trench coat with the long, snow-white hair and the smirk of an all-knowing being approached the judge and offered to take Will away from Stonehaven. When asked to reveal himself, the man simply introduced himself as Kite and just said that he would take responsibility for Will.

The court did everything but push Will to the strange man. However, the judge uncharacteristically resisted and demanded the man to leave, as Will could not leave Stonehaven for as long as the investigation continued.

The man approached the bench, the smirk still stuck to his face like a feather on a crow. The judge, now visibly angry and undeniably afraid, slammed his gavel once, twice, three times. However, before the gavel could hit a fourth time, the man clutched the judge's arm and mouthed something unintelligible into his ear. The judge's features dropped into an unreadable mask, and as if by some compulsion or spell, the judge just barely whispered, "Take him."

And with those simple words, Will no longer had control over his own life as he boarded a one-way ScotRail train to Edinburgh en-route to Dalkeith Palace. There, Will would find himself the newest resident of the Winchester House. A house that contained persons from every dirty alleyway and scurvy corner of Hell.

JASON BOND

Jason Bond, a Corpus Christi native, teaches fourth grade. He enjoys working outside, reading, and writing. He watches way too much television and knows way too much about 80s trivia. His latest novel, *Born Again*, will be available in 2021.

An excerpt from *Born Again*

A slight fog crawled across the backyard, starting low at the base of the trees. In late October, this was not uncommon, but this was summer. David looked up from his book to see the yard eerily engulfed. He squinted through the rapidly spreading gray mist. The steady wind that had been blowing all afternoon and cooling the bright afternoon sun had died down to nothing. The rapid weather change puzzled him.

He closed his book on his index finger to mark his page. Through the window, he saw his wife, Emily, in the house. She was scooping steaming vegetables into a serving bowl. David looked back to the yard. Where was his son?

"Nicky, come on in; dinner's about ready," David called into the thickening fog.

Then he spotted the small shape of his son spinning in circles and stumbling over the roots and grass, still playing with the toy bomber. David had trouble making out the edges and details of what he saw through the haze. The blue and white stripes of Nicky's shirt blurred in the darkness. Nicky, circling the tree, momentarily disappeared behind the thick oak trunk, causing David's heart to pound in his chest.

"Come on, son," David said sternly into the thickening soup. He was not using his "dad voice" yet, but there was a bit more authority behind his words. "Now!"

The ghostly shape in the fog ignored his command as it reappeared on the far side of the tree. Wispy gray vapors followed like a trail behind Nicky's tiny legs and arms as he continued to play. His two hands held the model as it dipped and dived through the still thickening fog.

"Come on," David mumbled to himself, frustrated. He pulled his "Read Like a Worm" bookmark from the rear pocket of his jeans and slid it between the pages, and then set the book down beside his iced tea and lemonade mixture, being careful not to let the condensation of the glass touch the paperback. David took another glance at Emily through the kitchen window to see if she had noticed the rapid weather change. She was still working diligently in the kitchen and was oblivious. His heart was racing. As he took the first steps off the porch, he could not help but feel that he was leaving the safety of the deck of a ship only to be entering the shark-infested waters below.

His first steps indeed broke through the thick gray fog like water. The ripples widened with each step.

He could no longer see his son.

"Nickolas Joseph Banister! You get yourself over here right now!" He could hear the tremble of doubt and terror in his words.

The spectral figure continued to circle the oak tree, going faster than before. Faster and faster until the blue and white stripes of his son's shirt blurred so David could no longer tell where it began and where it ended.

"Weather's getting worse, Hugo." Nicky's tiny voice echoed in the nothingness.

His son's voice seemed to come from more directions than one, echoing from all around.

"There is no turning back now, Charles!" Nicky shouted in a strange voice that was not his own.

David froze in mid-step, petrified halfway between the porch and the oak tree as his son raced non-stop around the tree, swishing his arms in the rising fog. Sweating, David tried to swallow but could not. His heart throbbed; his pulse quickened. He wanted to scream for his son to stop and run to him. He wanted to scoop his son into his arms and run inside to the safety of their home, but he could not. Afraid, powerless, all he could do was watch the surreal scene unfold before him. He was a slave to this moment.

"No! Don't do this!" Nicky shouted into the grayness of the fog. "Pull up! Pull up!" There was a desperation in his voice that could not have come from a five-year-old. The toy plane was a silver blur getting closer and closer to the thickness of the unforgiving ground below. Nicky was running as fast as he could, occasionally stumbling, still hypnotically circling the oak tree, and now holding the plane near his ankles just a few inches above the dirt.

David could just make out the face of his young son. Nicky was sweating profusely, and his fine hair was dripping wet against his forehead. Nicky's eyes were wide and unblinking as he stared at the cockpit of the model plane. The details faded away as little Nicky bent lower to guide the plane into the thickening fog below.

"No worries, pal, you will be fine without me," The strange voice replied.

Nicky's voice returned. "No. I won't! Pull up!"

The blur that was his son started to fade. The steady stream of blue and white became a memory. David's blood turned to ice.

JAVIER VILLARREAL

Javier Villarreal holds a BA and MA in Spanish from Pan American University, Edinburg, and a Ph.D. in Hispanic Linguistics from the University of Texas at Austin. His major fields of interests are Languages in Contact (Spanish and English), Mexican American Folklore, poetry, and photography. His works have been widely published. Javier retired from Texas A&M University-Corpus Christi in 2015. He resides in Corpus Christi with his family, where he writes, practices photography and promotes cultural events in South Texas.

Jim

Apenas amanece escucho
la incertidumbre de tus pasos
inquietar la serenidad del día.

Por la ventana te observo.
Atraviesas lento los huecos del camino,
melena y barbas libres en la brisa.

Andas pesado y vacilante
como anhelando a cada paso
recobrar algo perdido, algo olvidado.

Siempre sospechas que sea lunes,
como un eco detenido en la memoria
que reverbera en retirar la basura.

¿Cuántas veces naufragas
aferrado a un tambo de basura
para calmar esa obstinada pesadilla?

Lo arrastras hasta la calle solitaria
sobre hojas mustias y memorias desprendidas
reciclando escasos minutos de la vida.

Intransigente, te desvives divagando
como si llevaras a cuestas a un extraño,
en un incesante lunes obsesivo.

Acaso buscas en la repetición
de los pasos el atisbo de una luz
que despeje el artificio de los años.

A veces, en momentos fugitivos,
percibo albores entre la niebla
espesa de un rostro conocido.

-Hoy es lunes, Jim.
-Ahí viene el camión.

Te detienes, me miras de frente,
enlazas un pausado *How are you*
Luego, con los pies en la niebla, te alejas.

Jim

At first sign of dawn
the uncertainty of your movements
troubles the stillness of the day.

I see you from my window
plodding along your weathered driveway,
hair and beard ragged in the breeze.

Withdrawn in heavy footfalls
seemingly searching at every step
for something missing, something lost.

You always believe it's Monday,
a hardened echo in your mind
of garbage collection day.

How many times do you drift
back and forth clutching a trash bin
trying to calm an obstinate nightmare?

You drag it to the empty street
over faded memories, over fallen leaves,
recycling minutes from your past.

Unmoved, you labor along
as if shouldering a stranger's body
always on a stubborn Monday.

Perhaps you thirst
at every step for a glimpse of light
that could break the spell of time.

Sometimes, in fleeting moments,
I perceive a trace of clarity burning
through the heavy mist in your eyes.

-Today is Monday, Jim.
-Here comes the garbage truck.

You stop, stare into my eyes
and after a hesitant How are you?
fall back into the shadows

JIMMY WILLDEN

Jimmy Willden is an award-winning writer and filmmaker. He is also an American musician and composer. After beginning his career in music, he also forayed into journalism and filmmaking, winning several festival awards as director and screenwriter.

Beneath the Bowery, an excerpt from *Cameron, In Transit*

And so, finally, thirty-six excruciating crotch-pit-chafing blocks after my journey began, I now stand before The Bowery Electric, all out of breath; stumbling forth on feet, all out of steps.

It was a skip, but not nearly a hop, back when I began to notice the line. One person behind another person behind another, everybody averaging their ages together equaling ten years my junior. Blue hair, green hair, pink hair; with metal stabbed in cheeks or in noses or in eyebrows or in nipples or in wherever metal can be stabbed in, fashionably sending the message that with everybody behind everybody, each of their shits are too cool to stink.

My wondering brain registered this train of people standing before the old, looming building before them and me, and the only words that floated through all the data behind my eyes were, “Why are all these people here to see me?”

Moving the strap of my guitar case from my left shoulder, to my right, I bumble up to the door person, obviously nonbinary. The door person watches me with increasing displeasure as I approach and invade a little too much of their personal space, “May I help you?”

“Yeah, I’m playing here tonight.”

The door person holds a breath a little too long, and then exhales, “You -- are playing -- here?”

I glance down at my feet throbbing beneath me, then back up at the gatekeeper, “Right.”

The keeper of the gate sighs and stands, “Hold on.”

I watch as the door person disappears into the entryway beneath the blue and white neon sign, buzzing with the words Bowery Electric above the ever-growing train of rainbow hair and my obvious discomfort from the flames erupting within my bleeding ball-sack chafe.

Eventually, the all-powerful Bowery gatekeeper returns, with muted displeasure almost all the way ever-present, “Jason’s downstairs running sound check for Billy and Nora now. You can load in there.”

Confused and utterly lost in the here and now, I merely nod and walk through the entryway, hearing the neon words buzz above me. Directly to my left is the long, grungy bar beckoning me to come hither and drink from its blissful poison, and to my right, just through the entryway, are the stairs, one after the other, leading down into a darkness I'm not sure I want to explore. But I force myself to ignore the beckoning call from the beautiful booze behind the bar and move toward the staircase, swallowing down a burning anxiousness. Immediately, I'm stopped by a blob of a man with gigantic gauges shoved through stretched holes in his earlobes. He grunts through spittle sparkling on his lips, "You can't go down there."

The gatekeeper leans back, "Let him through. He's the opener."

Spittle-gauge man croaks, and a word slowly takes shape in the escaping tobacco-stained air, "Whaaaaaat."

"Yeah," says the gatekeeper, shrugging.

The spittle evolves into a full-fledged expanding line of wet, loogy-laced spit. I'm drawn to it like a moth to a flame, but in this case, like a small-town boy drawn to big city drool. He grunts again, lazily reaching for the chain between him and me, and unlatches it.

Gripping my guitar case strap for reassurance, I step down into the darkness of the stairwell and feel all that emerging heavy blackness engulf me, sending the machine in my chest into an overpumping overdrive. Breathing in and exhaling and breathing in again, I manage to take step after step down toward an elusive abyss beneath Bowery Street.

Below me, I hear the echoing groan of an old, rockabilly-toned electric guitar, thumping from a distant stand-up bass, snapping from some faraway snare drum, and the forever beautiful floating duet of male and female voices in harmonic unison, singing "Long Time Gone," the old Everly Brothers song. It wraps me in a warm embrace, and I take another step further down, nice and easy, leaving the other steps far above me. The anxiousness within melting away, I swim in the wonderful melody carrying me continuously toward the abyss. The singing continues. It's the same story as with so many songs. Love and loss.

I emerge into a vast, empty, poorly-lit room. Against the far wall, rises a wooden stage painted a dusty black, filled with a stripped-down drum set, and an old piano, nicked and worn from years of rock and roll abuse.

I find myself momentarily drawn to the drummer and his effortless time-keeping. His attention, though, is drawn elsewhere on stage. I follow his gaze, and my own eyes befall a woman with dark eyes and dark hair framing a soft but strong face. Her delicate fingers dance on the piano keys. As she continues to sing, she turns and smiles at a man standing with an old, black Gibson acoustic, with a five-point star painted into the center of its tuning head. The man matches the woman's dark features, and raises them at the River. His black hair haphazardly spiked up into an almost standing position, he perpetually resembles someone coming out of an ether fog. He leans forward and matches the woman's angelically floating melody with his own, floating merely an interval of a third beneath hers.

As they finish the song, I blink and swallow away whatever anxiety remains in my esophagus. "Who are you?" a voice calls out from somewhere behind me.

Turning in the direction of the seemingly disembodied voice, I find a small man with a shaved head and a dirty, tangled red beard hanging down to the center of his chest.

"I'm the opener," I say, anxiety churning within me all at once, all over again.

"We have an opener?"

Without anything else to do, I merely nod as if I know any better.

"Hey Jason," comes from the stage, from the man with the guitar. He grins, revealing one of his front teeth as chipped, as the red-bearded man gives him all of his attention.

"Yeah, Billy?"

"Can you give me a little more of Nora in my wedge? It's getting a little muddy up here."

"Of course, Billy," obliges Jason as he nods, sending his long ginger beard into an excited, swinging motion. He leans into the sound booth and turns a knob on the massive mixing board that's about a generation out-of-date.

As Billy turns back to the woman on stage, he mouths something to her, and they both laugh.

"What's your name?"

My attention back on ginger-bearded Jason, I cough, "Ca-Cameron."

"Cacameron?"

"Minus the first Cah."

Jason fishes his cell phone from one of the ocean-size pockets of his massive cargo shorts, dials random numbers, and places the phone to his ear just as the band starts another song full of magic from generations ago. He stuffs a finger into his other ear and turns away from the stage, trying in vain to hear the elusive whoever on the other end of the line a little better, as Billy and Nora launch into another beautiful harmony of "Oh So Many Years," another haunting song by the Everly Brothers.

"Hey, Cacameron!" Jason yells, harshly breaking through the sonic perfection enveloping me once more. Returning my attention to him, the look on his face reveals his judgment that I'm just another one of the many fuck-ups who fuck up his sound checks. "You're in the wrong place, man. You're playing on the small stage, upstairs. You can't be down here."

"Oh," is all I can say before he ushers me back up the stairs, back from where I came. As I ascend with each step, Billy and Nora continue their game of capturing magic in music from below me, singing. And then, just as the music fades away along with the abyss beneath, I am once again anchored above ground. I wasn't supposed to be alone; I wasn't supposed to be trusted to be left alone with myself only in this gigantic city full of shattered hopes and broken dreams.

Yet, here I am -- all alone, all at once -- all by my lonesome self.

JOANN SANDERSON

JoAnn Sanderson was born in Iowa, received a Master's degree in English Education at Southern Illinois University, and taught in Illinois public schools for many years. After she retired, she researched possible places to re-locate and chose Corpus Christi, Texas.

Clean-Spirited

As I lay on the sofa in the living room of the large three-storied house, which had been subdivided to accommodate apartments for retired seniors, I looked alternately toward the tv screen and down at the book on my lap. Beside me on the sofa's cushions, I had propped a box of Kleenex. I had no idea what movie was showing on the screen or the meaning of the words written in the book I was trying to read. Looking as miserable as I felt, I lay listlessly in baggy jogging pants, yesterday's make-up, and two hair curlers perched on top of my head. For over two hours, I had been recalling and regretting the words I had spewed at Alice. I had shouted at her, "Alice, I am fed up with your meticulous, intrusive, O.C.D. cleaning! If I wanted to live in the Hill Crest Sanatorium across town, I would check myself in there and let Medicare help me pay the rent!" Surely, I had made a mess of it.

I could still see her face when I shouted at her. I could still hear her soft, pitiful, "But, Maggie, I was only trying to. . . ," and my interrupting her, "Yes, I know, to help me. Help me do what? Hasten my commitment to the looney bin? After I come into the house and wipe my feet on the door mat, you shake the mat outside and clean the hallway with the Swiffer. If I'm drinking a cup of coffee, you watch me until I take the last sip and put the cup down. Then you whisk it away, take it to the kitchen, wash it, dry it, and put it on the second shelf, third cup on the left in the cabinet. You wipe the knobs on the outside of all our bedrooms with Clorox, claiming that the outside of the doors is community property and should be germ-free. Do you know what happens to people who have no contact with germs? They die, Alice, they die!" Alice looked down at the floor, tugged at the hem of her cardigan sweater, turned, and shuffled slowly to her room.

Awash in my remorse, I heard Sylvia enter the room. Why did it have to be Sylvia? I wanted to talk with Rosie, who would listen and then offer to take me to Bert's Bingorama, or Kareem, who would listen and then slip out a flask from his pocket to pour me a swig of his doctor-prescribed medication, or Constantine, who would listen and then click on a deep sleep meditation on a smartphone app he had downloaded.

But Sylvia? Sylvia always brought out the meanness inside me. She walked past me, ignoring my weak, "Hey, Sylvia," and sat down primly on the chair beside the sofa. No response was Sylvia's style. The others admire her. I have to agree she's beautiful. They tell her, and each other, how well she looks for her age. They obsequiously "ooh and ahh" over her soft, silver hair. They don't realize that they are implying that the rest of us with coarse grey hair or no hair on our heads, maneuvering about with wheelchairs and walkers, have not "aged well."

It is obvious why she has aged so well. While the other tenants share the responsibilities of keeping up the house, she does nothing. Despite my complaining, they obligingly take up the slack. Others think she is beautiful, graceful, and self-assured. I think she is beautiful, uppity, and disdainful.

I saw Sylvia glance at me. But did she acknowledge my woeful appearance? Did she offer some semblance of comfort? Of course not. She had a rapport, a camaraderie with the others, but not with me. Rosie, Kareem, and Constantine thought she was charming. But I thought she used her charm to manipulate others to satisfy her need for attention and admiration.

However, since she had entered the living room and had primly settled into the chair, I had not been thinking about my transgression against Alice. I became preoccupied with thinking about Sylvia's deficiencies. I began to realize that my remorse indicated my moral compass was leading me to higher ground. I, at least, have acknowledged my impropriety, if only to myself. If Sylvia had treated a friend in a hostile, nasty manner, she wouldn't lie on a couch, moaning and groaning, regretting her obnoxious behavior. She would be oblivious to her reprehensible behavior. If not oblivious, indifferent. She wouldn't undergo a change of heart and repent, need the comfort of others. She would go haughtily about her business.

Compassion? Humility? Not beautiful, selfish Sylvia. But there was hope for me! If I could talk with a sympathetic listener, I would move along on the road to recovery. But there sat aloof Sylvia.

In spite of what I knew about Sylvia, despite how I resented her presence in this house, I spilled out the whole story to her about what had happened between Alice and me—every gut-wrenching detail. I sobbed and blew my nose several times in the telling, wadding Kleenex tissues and dropping them on the floor.

When I stopped talking, Sylvia left the chair and sauntered past the tv screen. After I hurled my book toward her (but not at her because I am not a physically violent person), she turned toward me and released a prolonged defensive hiss. "Get away from me, you feckless feline. Go to the kitchen and slurp your saucer of milk before I throw it out the back door," I shouted. "And don't even think about coming back in here and jumping into my lap, expecting me to apologize."

Sylvia shot toward the kitchen, and, exhausted, I fell asleep on the sofa. When I woke up several hours later, Sylvia was on my lap, purring. The wadded Kleenex tissues I had dropped on the floor had disappeared, and the book I had thrown had been closed and placed on the center of the coffee table in front of the sofa. The tv was turned off, and I smelled the familiar scent of Clorox permeating the room.

JOEL ORTIZ

Joel Jay Ortiz has been reading, writing, and performing poetry since 1991. He started at various open mikes, reading poetry with musicians, and then continued when open mike with spoken word began appearing.

Death

Working is for stiffs. These pictures I take every day, these computer chips, getting to me, typing with my fingers takes so much energy. My skin is cold, with millions of goose pimples covering my body. Someone once told me when you get chills like this, it's because there's someone walking over your grave. This person has never been sick, not like this, not like me. Look at that guy, my manager; I need to talk to him. I need to get out of here. It's been eight hours, and I don't feel so well.

Michelle, the pretty little milf, looks at me and asks if I'm okay. Her perfume, some expensive brand made to turn on men with their base pheromones, just makes me wretch.

I run to the restroom with my head wet with sweat and fall to my knees. That last smell from Michelle's breast or breath or perfume smells like the worst trash to me, makes me lean down and place my hand on the edge of the toilet rim, not caring who used it last or who cleaned up and flushed.

Nothing comes out because there is nothing in my stomach. I talk to the monsters, spit dribbling out of my mouth, my nose running, long trails of snot-dripping into the dirty toilet, goose pimples up and down. I'm so cold, but I'm sweating as if I'm stuck in a sauna., I just need a little taste.

After about fifteen minutes of losing it, I go back to my job of taking pictures. Richard, my stupid manager who always likes to give me lectures on tardiness and absences, asks if I'm doing okay.

"No," I manage weakly to say.

"Can you work the rest of your shift? You have been leaving quite early a lot recently. Is there something you would like to talk about? You know we are here for you."

I listen to his speech, and I know where he is going with this lecture. Little skeletons dance in his pupils. Beyond his eyes, behind him, I see a couple of my co-workers, and they are looking at me funny. I know they are talking about me, just like Rich here is talking about me, in a way that he wants to tell me something, but he can't quite get it out. So, he beats around the bush, to use the thousand-year-old cliché. How many thousands of years have people been trying to say one thing when they really wanted to say something else entirely, a completely different thought than what was conveyed. The subconscious, the sublime, and my manager want to talk about my problem, but all that oozes out is 'problem.'

Rich's coffee-tinged bad breath makes me think of all the dirty sewers and dirtiest toilet bowls, and I make this retching noise with my mouth as if I was going to throw up right there in front of him. It is loud and surprising. He looks at me with fear. Michelle has a look of disgust painted all over her pretty china doll face. I retch again and run to the restroom.

As I'm kneeling at the toilet bowl, Richard comes in and asks if I am feeling okay. Again, with the stupid questions. After hearing me for a couple of more talks with the monsters, Richard says simply, "Ivan, if you need to go home, go right on ahead. Go ahead and take the next day off as well, but I expect you to be here Friday, okay, don't let me down. C'mon Ivan, go home and get some rest. You don't sound so good."

It's like I get well for a second as I wipe away the tears from my eyes. That Rich, he's such a good man, I keep taking advantage of him, and he always gives me the benefit of the doubt.

I clock out at the machine and retrieve my empty bag from my locker. I slap the bag over my shoulder and leave that cold building. It is early morning, about 7:00 am. I have been working ten hours straight, and I am really sick. The traffic smells really get to me. I immediately set my hands on my knees and vomit. This time something comes up. It is this world, with its natural smells of oil and gasoline filling the streets. The odors of the sewer mixing with the trees mixing with dumpster mixing with perfume are too much for my guts. The morning dew, the dumpster, car exhaust, doggie-doo-doo, her hair, my bad B.O., it all comes up with the sniff of the real world, and when it comes up, it burns all the way up my throat as I spit out the bile that I had deep in my system. It is white when it hits the sidewalk, and I hear it sizzle so early this morning.

I manage to finally get over this predicament and find my way back home. I get in the door and immediately drop my pants and take off my shirt. Cold, in my boxers, I go to my room and get underneath my heavy covers. It is wintertime, and I am under one of my favorite covers, a blanket that I had for over ten years given to me by this old girlfriend of mine. I don't know why I hold on to it when I no longer have any contact with her, but I can't throw this old and tattered blanket away. We had both been discarded and lived through so much life together; I just could never get rid of it. I get under the velvet cover and pass out to nerve-shaking nightmares.

On a boat, in the middle of the ocean with rain falling over me, waves trying to capsize my boat, and I'm shivering in this Arctic Circle, looking for heat in all these freezing temperatures. I'm lost for years in the northern seas, freezing my heart all alone, with not even a deckhand to alleviate my loneliness nor to help me remember what warmth was.

I wake up with sweat-soaked sheets stuck to my cold skin. I peel them off and throw them on the floor. The clock tells me I was asleep for only twenty minutes, and I can't sleep anymore.

The phone rings. Veronica asks how I was doing, and I tell her not so well.

She asks if she can come over. She had just visited Chuy and says she bought some oatmeal crème pies 'would you like some.' That dirty water, that Texas T, that dragon she is bringing wakes me out of my stupor. Just knowing she's coming over makes my sickness heel a little bit.

It's true I love the dragon, but Veronica is my true love. Veronica I met when I was still in high school, in my Italian class. I was trying to learn Italian to read Calvino, but all it ever did was get me more confused within my English tongue. But Veronica was in my class, sitting next to me. A very beautiful woman, she had me breathing every time she spoke to me. We started to hang out after school, and eventually, we became an item. Unfortunately, when I left for school, she stayed behind, and we drifted apart, but upon my graduation from the university, I began to experiment with some drugs until I found one that was to my liking. When I came back home, the dragon was always on my mind until I found Veronica again. It was a quaint existence together. We did everything together. She lived with me off and on; sometimes, when we get too crazy on the dragon, she would go back to her stepmother's, but lots of times, we struggled together.

She's been out of town to visit her real mother in Houston. She had some methadone with her for her trip, but now since she's back home, she wanted the real stuff. Unbeknownst to me, she had gone to our dealer's and picked up some dope for the both of us. My nose stops running, and my bones stop aching. I go to the restroom and get out my works.

In an old cellular phone case, black leather, I unzip it. It consists of a bottle cap, already dirty with remnants and traces up and down the cooker. There is a little makeshift handle to hold it. There are a few Q tips, a lighter, of course, and last but not least, a needle.

I expect her in fifteen minutes, but after thirty minutes, I call. She says she's on the way. I sit there on my couch, cold as hell and feeling very sick. I try closing my eyes, try to fall asleep, but sleep never comes. Every time my eyes close, strange faces appear. Great big, horrid figures with teeth sharp and eyes dark as dense forests, where monkeys live and yell, screaming at the moon, these faces, these harbingers of doom and terror live in that darkness when my lids are closed. I open my eyes, sweating on the leather couch, with my skin stuck on the leather, feeling like melted saran wrap on my skin. So uncomfortable, I try to sit on a blanket, but my sweat keeps making noises on this skin of the couch.

The television holds no relief either. It's nothing but talk shows of who is whose daddy and how my daddy beat me when I was a child or mock court shows where people are suing other people over parking in the wrong space. I flip the channels for about ten minutes until I finally turn the sad television off. Nothing.

I call one hour after Veronica first called, and this time no answer. The harlot. Where could she be? Who is she with? I know she's with someone, doing my dope. She's out there sucking someone off. She's in somebody's trailer dancing or in the back of some car with her panties on the floor. I bet she's on some bed getting drilled, and well, here I am sick as a dog, waiting for this, this, damn that, Veronica. Why won't she hurry up? I love Veronica, and I love what she has for me. Both of these warmths that make me feel good about myself. Those two warmths that give me confidence, I need them right now, right here.

Ring ring goes the phone. Is it my dope, is the only racing thought through my sick mind. It's Veronica. She got tied up, so she says. By whom, I wonder? But she eases my heart by saying she will be here in a few minutes. She's just down the street. Get everything ready, she tells me, and I tell her I already have, and now the time I've been waiting for is so long, but so short.

I hear her car outside my window. I already have the door unlocked. She comes in like nothing. Places her bags on the couch. She comes to me and kisses me, but her kisses leave me so weak. Where's it at? are the only words I have for her. She digs in her pocket, like a drill in the earth, looking for oil, and in her tight pocket, she pulls out a balloon. A pretty good red balloon, larger than usual. She throws it to me, and I unwrap it on our coffee table. I have a shot glass of water, a cooker, my lighter, and two needles set on the coffee table, sans the coffee, sans the big books.

Busting the red balloon, I let obsidian tar fall onto my cooker. It is a big piece of tar. It bubbles up after about thirty seconds of flame underneath it, and my guts begin to boil along with it. That smell of the drug rises up from the spoon and hits my nostrils. Immediately I want to throw up again. I start to retch, but I stop myself because I don't want to spill any of the drug on the floor.

I draw up about seventy-five units of complete darkness. She sits next to me. It is dark in that syringe, and it looks like the depths of the deepest oceans.

"Hit me first," she says, holding on to my arm, squeezing it tight.

"You know I always do, baby."

I look in her face, and she is looking at the point where the needle is about to enter her. "Come on," she whispers.

Her eyes flutter as I push the plunger. Her arm falls limply between her legs. Her mouth opens wide as she falls back on the black leather couch.

Maybe it's too much, but let me find out on my own. Veronica, mummy-like, on the leather couch, lies there unresponsive. I pick up my needle, wishing to be on her level of highness. With my queen, my princess. I just follow the rest of my scar tissue. A joke enters my mind, of the two greatest inventions in the world. Heroin and the hypodermic syringe. Cracking a smile, I push the drug into my vein.

My eyes get heavy. I close them, thinking of the rush; it feels so great. Better than sex, better than orgasms. It's warm, enveloping. Better than food, better than water on a hot day, hot and overwhelming. I can't remember if I remember anything at all, but my eyes close quickly. That's the only truth because when truth is found, it comes the quickest.

There's no holding Veronica, no taking out the flowers, but numbness. Beyond clouds. In dark shapes coloring my vision. Blackness comes on so quick. This nothing, where hearts are not next to loved ones. Alone in this void, this is what I've become. Nothing but dust, nothing but dirt, but...

JOSEPH WILSON

Joseph Wilson taught Senior English Advanced Placement, Film Studies, and Creative Writing at Richard King High School for 42 years.

Things We Did and Did Not Do

We bump into Tina B. in the line for the movie
After we trade compliments
Tina says she bet her daughter
Who is saving seats inside
That she would know five fellow film patrons

She had already won when I kissed her on the cheek
"…a drink after?"
"…no, no, I'm running at 7"
After watching "Parasite" with my old roommate Joe H.
After an animated discussion at the wine bar until one

About current wives, our work, the waitress's intricately woven dress
Jazz, mistakes of karmic proportions, sons, ex-wives
About the swirling blue currents
That shape the vicissitudes of our lives
We have quiet talk at his house over iced cold water

About the patent lunacy of Trump
And the ever-looming election
And how Joe's daughter looks
So so much like his second wife
We share a few secrets and a long goodnight hug

While driving home I listen to Ed Sheeran
Sing about how he will always remember
Being kissed by a woman under a lamppost on 6th Street
I kissed a woman there once too
When we pulled to a stop on Bee Cave Road

I didn't love her but I wanted to love her
And now I can't remember her last name
Later on Facebook I write my movie review and
Then I read the Times op-eds until 3

After sleeping in to 9

I mow the front yard and the back yard
I play with the poodle puppies on the stone patio
The fuzzy faced one unties my boots
And bites my nose when I hold her close
In the pasture I finish the mowing

And then I move the winter debris to the back fence line
Then I hang a prayer flag for my mother
I cut red winter roses for my desk
Where in three hours the aroma
Will nearly intoxicate me

And Then I Fell

Two spilled drinks
Misunderstood signals
Sugar-filled promises
Heightened expectations
Hubris
Hope
Too much grass
Not enough green
The look from the way up
The vision from the top down
A history of loss
So much joy
Too much pain

My grip was not strong enough
I held on far too long
Past injuries
Fear of the bleak known
Fear of the sweet unknown
My father's rejection and my mother's tight love
The need of family connection
Weak ankles because of basketball
Discontent
Enlightenment
A redhead
Good champagne
Another redhead

The conundrums of Christianity
The lust I carry for those who speak in witty sentences
Olives stuffed with blue cheese
The intoxication of art
A good woman with pretty eyes
A smart woman with dark eyes
Green eyes
Guilt
Simple betrayal
When push came to shove
Her tee shirt on a cold cold night
Bagels with lox and cream cheese
Vodka neat

Listening to a Fugue by Bach Arranged by Mozart

So I am listening to my new cd over lunch at my desk
Bach Fugues by Emerson String Quartet
Or what the average person might say
Boring boring boring
Written by a long dead white guy
Played by four almost dead white guys in dark suits with goatees and black glasses

Esther sweeps into the room to give me her cell number
Bends over and writes it on a stickie in red water base marker
She is a substitute teacher now
Previously the daughter-in-law of a neighbor
An artist who conceived of and created a mosaic table that resides in my sitting room
Currently a beautiful really beautiful smart talented single woman finding herself

As she leaves, she cocks her head
Eyes raised to the speaker
"Nice, I like it"
The fugues were conceived by Papa Bach for the keyboard
For his young second wife to learn to play the instrument better
How much he must have adored his lovely Anna Magdelena

To create such beautiful melodic forms then to repeat
The basic sound elements
And then to invent variations
On his so exquisite themes
Did I mention counterpoint
Music imitates life with structure/repetition/variation/collision

In random order
As I muse on this idea a colleague knocks and walks in
And asks if I might read her daughter's breakup poetry
Before I answer she asks "Who is this?"
When I say "Bach"
She responds with "Ah"

The word arcing up as a forward pitching yes

Like a balloon cut from a string
Ascending
As she leaves she mentions in almost an aside
"I lost all my music in the divorce"
Only 50 years after his death Bach's music

Was virtually unknown
His discarded manuscripts became fish wrappings
When young Mozart was introduced by a friend
To the long dead and forgotten compositions
He liked it
He liked it so much that he transcribed The Well-Tempered Clavier

Into music for strings
As I listen just this moment
I think about four piece bands
A kind of declared union
Really a marriage of true musical minds
I think about marriages held together bv fraying strings

I think about the poem my friend just gave me ten minutes ago
That chronicles the severance of a relationship
Where once-shared aspirations exploded in slowing motion
But if you must ask me to comment about the music
Let me say directly
I love it

JOHN MEZA

John Meza writes poems—and builds bridges. Most Sundays he helps feed the homeless people in Artesian Park in Corpus Christi. A powerful speaker, he often reads his work at open mics and other events.

I Asked Her Why

I asked her why

She was coloring

The tortilla

She said

There was a

Picture of Jesus

On it.....

I told her

To use

The burnt sienna

Crayon for

The skin

No one ever uses

The burnt sienna

Every Day I Climb

Poetry/photo John Meza

Graphic layout William Mays

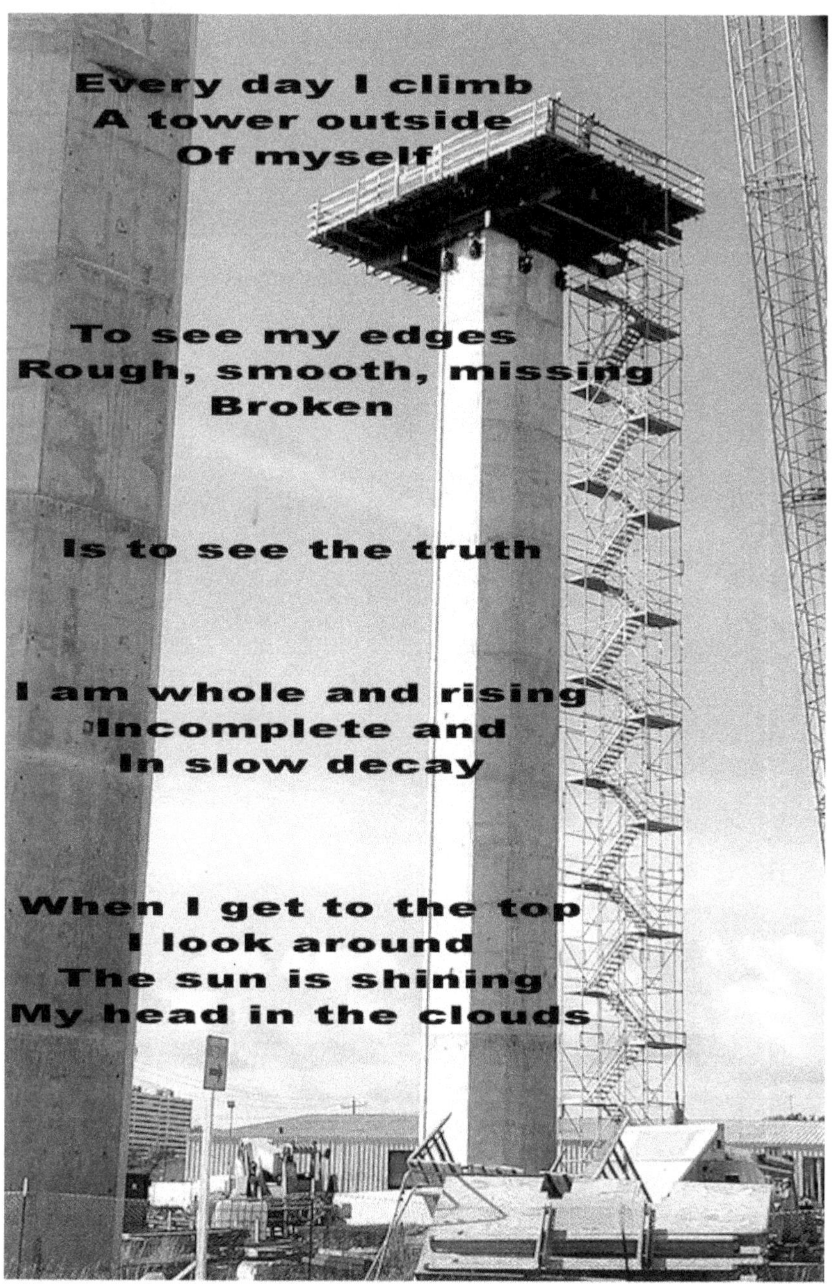

JOHN PETTIGROVE

A retired physician, John Pettigrove has been fishing all his life. His book *Run of the Tide* will be available in 2022. Here's an excerpt.

Excerpt from *Run of the Tide*

Two hundred years ago, aboriginal peoples along the Texas Gulf Coast were known as Karankawa or "Karankaway." They were said to be a barbarous people and were widely feared by early Texas settlers. They were barbarous, yes, but they lived as one with nature. Few other men had the strength to even string a Karankawa bow. Old-time settlers recounted seeing Karankawa hunters gliding silently through the water hunting for Redfish and Black Drum, sensing the fish in the water just from the vibrations and sounds they made on the flats.

They had lived and hunted on the Gulf coast for hundreds if not thousands of years before the Europeans came. They loved their lives and wanted no other. Modernity damned them for this. Now they are gone. But the Karankawa's passion lives within us. What was once their passion has become ours, and through our lives, they live again on their beloved bays and flats.

Sight fishing is hunting in a most ancient and primitive way. It is an aesthetic experience that unites us with that spirit of human existence as it was lived millennia ago. It is a mystery that puts us in touch with people long gone from this earth and allows us to see the world as it once might have been. There is purity and innocence about angling. Long dormant passions awaken in us, and we become at once exhilarated and united with some distant past.

Modernity denies the relevance of such experience. Since the nineteen fifties, scientists say we have been living in a new geologic epoch called the Anthropocene, where geologically significant conditions and processes are profoundly altered by human activity. The world is changing rapidly, some say irrevocably. Angling gives us the experience of seeing the world as it once was.

What we now call Texas was once just a blank spot on a map at the limits of the known world. It was one of the dark places of the Earth inhabited by a fierce race, just as ancient Britain and Europe were when my ancestors haunted the Roman frontier.

The Spaniards and early settlers had little regard for the coastal tribes. They considered them savage cannibals who danced in fiery fandangos or sulked in the dunes, inspiring fear and dread. The Karankawa, the Copane, the Malaquite, and the Aranama from which so many of our bays and estuaries take their name are long gone from this country.

We don't know much about those early native coastal people. We can only guess about the millennia between the last great ice age and the sixteenth and seventeenth centuries when the first Europeans began arriving. Cabeza de Vaca's account of his shipwreck on the Texas Coast during the early sixteenth century is one of very few extant records of the Texas coastal tribes at the time of the Spanish conquest. While great material cultures arose in the Valley of Mexico and in the Yucatan, it would seem that life along the Texas Coast had not changed from the earliest prehistoric times. But with the coming of the Europeans, everything changed. Even before most Native Americans ever saw a European, the white man's diseases decimated them. Early mariners and the conquistadors themselves imported savage epidemics among people who had no immunity to even measles, let alone the dreaded smallpox.

JOSHUA BRIDGWATER HAMILTON

Joshua Bridgwater Hamilton is a Louisville, KY native who migrated to Corpus Christi with his family. Between Kentucky and Texas, he has traveled and lived in several places, including Spain, Appalachia, Panamá, Peru, the Philippines, and the Colorado River. Currently, he is an MFA candidate at Texas State University. He has two chapbooks: *Rain Minnows* (Gnashing Teeth Publishing) and *Slow Wind* (Finishing Line Press). His poetry appears in such journals as *Windward Review*, *Driftwood*, *Voices de la Luna*, *Tiny Seed Journal*, *Sybil Journal*, and *San Antonio Review*. www.joshuabridgwaterhamilton.com

Song for Misspent Youth

I ate my own desire. There where
the mirror reflected fruits, vines,
a sickening pace to rot faster
until the motorcycle slipped
completely off the road. No more
glass dance, the mortgage melted
in my hands, blindingly free
and anchor-less. One more dog-
dripped bark at a pinking moon
and you folded yourself up
in denim forever. The wind
bends trees walls cars sideways
through prism of salt crystal
prescience, reads the future
homeless sweating and grimed
planting colorful tents
along scythe-curved stretch of beach.
Make this space for the incorrect
calculation, the botched theory
thousands live by, follow the line
into pavement, dust, cotton bolls,
build beginnings again
from slant sun-ray 2x4s
and the mortar squeezed
from desperation.

A Hundred Years

Before Walter leaves the house
for the Louisville L&N train station,
he sits in the den reading the paper
in an olive armchair.
Lady B fixes him eggs, a rasher of bacon,
and hot tea, asks him about the war,
last night's Reds game, or the Beetle Bailey
comic strip. The responses are simple,
heartfelt. Her offerings speak gratitudes,
parse love into the enameled pan
and simmer with the warm oven.

Their eldest daughter lives in New Orleans,
sends letters and jazz records – the spirits
of Preservation Hall cut into vinyl
and jumping with a metal tide.
Vines of music slink from the parlor speakers
in the evening, charging the mind.
But too often the tinny world clicks and pulses
through the receiver tubes with an accidental,
irrelevant glow – a wallpaper
that asks too much of the inhabitants.

Their youngest daughter lives in Maine
with three kids and a husband
somewhere in the the Gulf of Tonkin.
She calls Lady B on the phone, talks about
movies seen with the kids, chattering
a dustcloud around her personal matters:
John Wayne's epic, single-handed battles,
sweeping cinematics of lonely horse country—
she likes to linger on the supple,
dancing ligature of horse and rider. Lady B
easily imagines these captivating pantomines,
the seduction of an exaggerated solitude,
a real national hero. But she finds the Bible
more graceful:
epic storms and destruction
laced by love stories
like spidery writing cut into rock
with pounding surf.

To live a hundred years, she once told me,
you must know the insignificance
of even one more year,
the pettiness
of a greener dress whose pleats
tumble like rivulets,
of another appliance that opens
new kitchen mysteries,
of the little coffin nailed shut
within a plump retirement plan.
Give freely of your own graces,
expecting from tomorrow
nothing more than tomorrow.

Tools for Waking the Dreamer

Peculiar to states
of vast freedom
our movement unspools routes
plentiful and jumbled
from sun-baked gps

through Georgia's
inherited fields,
the Smokies' blue haze,
the stark Rockies
and roads West, then later

straight off into yonders
where the lens of wealth
pretends not to focus, the subject
feeling identity
even freer to form —

ill-defined journeys
remembered by few details —
dreamlike filters
applied to the whole of life
and leading backwards: waking up
to say "What happened?" Thinking

of a stained plush bear — once the color
of snow, nose chewed off, burrowing
in the warm crook of late
afternoon beds; plastic trilogy

of Lego towers, randomly bricked
yellow — red — blue — white, snapping
Saturday morning sun into modular
cuts and flows of pleasure;

natatorium, long arc into cold water
before dawn, dread sense
in Dagobah swamp,

son's intuition
darkened to discipline,

shadow father slinging
blazing arcs
as son thrashes
below wavy
aquamarine—

deadly threats
lurk in blind spots, hide
their parallel dimensions
within age-baked densities –

the chipped plastic blocks
form road markers totemed
into shape of movement,
track the benevolence
of primary colors
past bear season's plush comfort
into quartz chiclet of chlorine—

unfathomable, total, simple.

That sun-tattered sentence
opens up, finger-stained in the hour
of early dirt, its one thin sentence
of gold and onyx hope
persistent
no matter pages

turned — growing sense
of freefall suddenly
waking the reader

to see the line of ink crisping
on the long skin of humanity.

WRITER'S BLOCK

GRAPHIC WILLIAM MAYS

TITLE CAROL MAYS

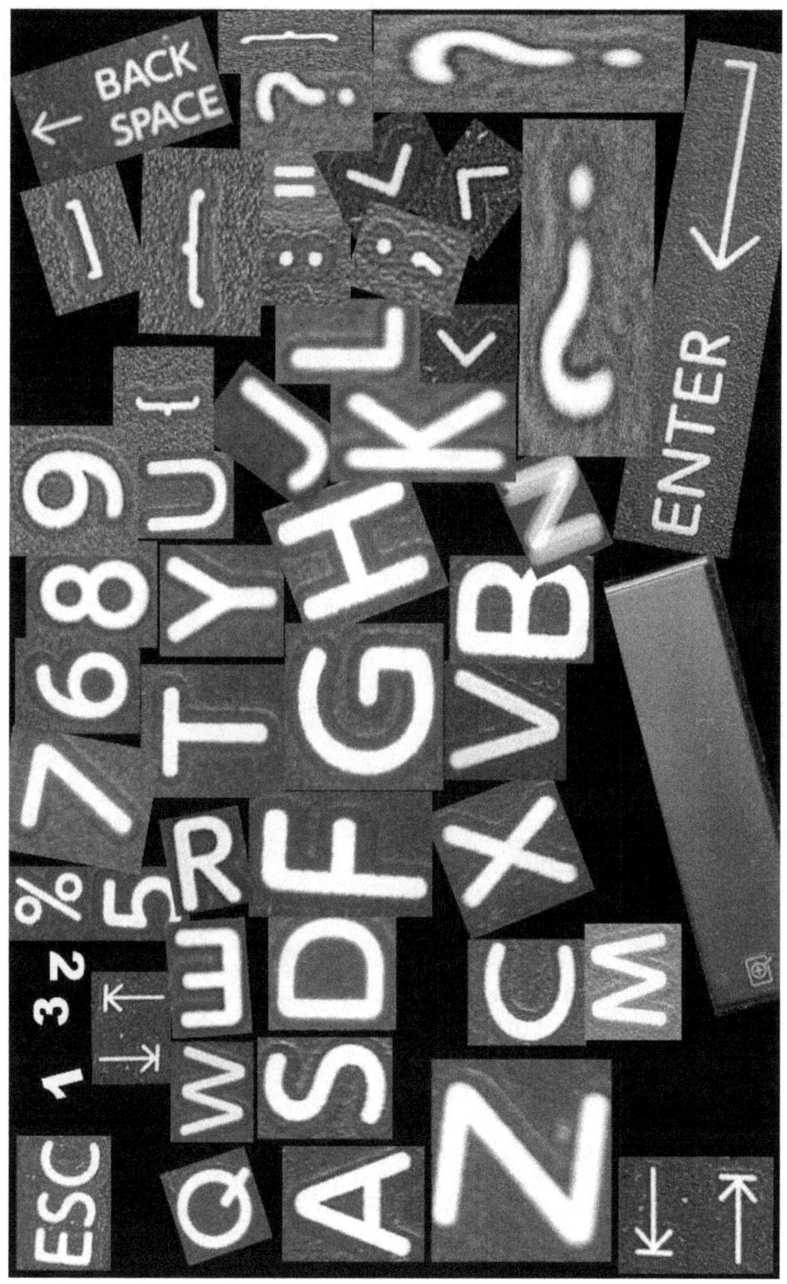

JUAN PEREZ

Juan Manuel Pérez, a Mexican-American poet of indigenous descent and a Poet Laureate for Corpus Christi, Texas (2019-2020), is the author of several books of poetry including, SCREW THE WALL! AND OTHER BROWN PEOPLE POEMS (FlowerSong Books, 2020). The award-winning poet, history teacher, and Pushcart Nominee, is also a member of the Horror Writers Association, the Science Fiction Poetry Association, and the Military Writers Society of America. Juan worships his Creator and chases chupacabras in the South Texas Coastal Bend Area.

The Great Whataburger Speaks To Its Lover

Corpus Christi, Texas 2013

O' pace yourself thy lover, pace yourself
for with my name they have consecrated
tall buildings and beautiful, baseball fields
even pretty shrines where I'm created

O' pace yourself thy lover, pace yourself
for only I can satisfy hunger
for only I can take you to places
where your empty belly will not monger

O' pace yourself thy lover, pace yourself
with a Patty Melt, Chocolate Shake, and Fries
or a Honey Butter Chicken Biscuit
with Onion Rings and box of Apple Pie

O' pace yourself thy lover, pace yourself
for there is much more of me to enjoy

GOD'S Train

Daydreaming one sunny afternoon while listening to celloist Susan Sturman play and Alan Berecka read from his chapbook, "The Fall Of The Leaf Suite," in unison at Del Mar College in 2018.

clackity clack
clackity clack [train whistle]
clackity clack
clackity clack [train whistle]

fall
falling
fallen
eternal
scream
screaming
screamed
space
spacing
spaced between
my eyes
my ears
my brains
my thoughts
between
the past
the here
the now
the future
will it last?
make it last

clackity clack
clackity clack [train whistle]
clackity clack
clackity clack [train whistle]

like leaves
in the fall
falling
fallen

in the cool autumn
like men fall
falling
fallen
bleed
bleeding
bled their last breath
slow
death
march
into eternity
men rise and fall
rising and falling
rose and fell
again
again
again

clackity clack
clackity clack [train whistle]
clackity clack
clackity clack [train whistle]

live
living
lived like supple tulips in spring
leave
leaving
left skeletons for the hungry earth
always
once
upon this time
again
again
again
eternal fall
falling
fallen
space
spacing
spaced between
suns and planets
sons and fathers
creator and created

simple you and me

clackity clack
clackity clack   [train whistle]
clackity clack
clackity clack   [train whistle]

soft beats
soft beats
like soft feet
footsteps
like soft rain
on the hot tin roof
smile brother
it hasn't rained in a while
rain-steps chasing the dryness
of our intrepid
fall
falling
fallen souls
only GOD picks you up
only GOD picks you up
only GOD picks us all up

clackity clack
clackity clack   [train whistle]
clackity clack
clackity clack   [train whistle]

the train of eternity is coming for us
the cosmic smoke-stack signals the presence
the deep whistle like no other on earth
is in fact the herald sound of heaven
ready or not, GOD's train just came in
are you getting on? …or not?
either way
it will cycle again
picking up the next set
ready for eternity
come on… are you getting on?
the wheels begin to move forward

clackity clack
clackity clack [train whistle]

clackity clack
clackity clack [train whistle]

with the beat
the beat
the beat
the heartbeat
that beats
within you
your soul
your mind
your thoughts
between the space
between the ears
between the sun
and the earth
beating
and beating
and beating
between you
and GOD's words

clackity clack
clackity clack [train whistle]
clackity clack
clackity clack [train whistle]

the conductor smiles
waves goodbye for now
wait… was that Jesus?
HE'll be back
HE promised
HE settles back
into the conductor's space
and you decide to wave back
now at the emptiness
of a closed window
and the strong sound of train wheels

clackity clack
clackity clack [train whistle]
clackity clack
clackity clack [train whistle]

fall
falling
fallen
HE will catch you too
HE promised HE would...
soon
you'll get on that train…
soon
not now
but soon… enough

clackity clack
clackity clack [train whistle]
clackity clack
clackity clack [train whistle]

KAREN CLINE TARDIFF

Karen's works can be seen in several literary magazines and websites. She founded the Aransas County Poetry Society and hosts a monthly Open Mic in Rockport, Texas. She has a Kindle edition book of poetry, *Stumbling to Breathe*. She is the Editor-in-Chief of Gnashing Teeth Publishing.

Holy Communion

Holy is the small gap between his front teeth, where my name lounges before sliding out of his prophesying mouth. Holy is the way his hair stubbles around his jaw, above his lips, on his crown. Holy is the clavicle I reach for when he is above me in all his glory. Holy is the sweat which baptizes our bodies, writhing in holy communion. Holy is his name, as I scream it to the heavens. Holy is the moment, when gods meet us at our little death.

Forgotten Gods

Now is when he is rising,
tending to the day's chores.
Standing naked before the sun,
he bathes himself in the river.

Tending to the day's chores
he reflects on what is left undone.
He bathes himself in the river
where the earth empties into the sea.

He reflects: on what is left undone,
the ways of man, forgotten gods,
where the earth empties into the sea.
He is radiant in the sunlight.

The ways of man; forgotten gods
standing naked before the sun-
He is radiant in the sunlight.
Now is when he is rising.

How To Walk and Chew Bubblegum at the Same Time

Double Bubble is the chunky gum in an
individual wrapper that is fun to say.
The accountant Walter Diemer spent his
spare time perfecting the bubble gum
recipe we all know and love today.
Fleer Chewing Gum Company wanted
a gum for blowing bubbles, but it was
their very own accountant who put
the bubble in the gum years later.
I imagine Walter, thin tie and thinner
moustache, in a drafty basement in
Philadelphia on a workbench beside
the old coal-fired heating system, his
wife upstairs rolling her eyes while
she sipped bootleg gin and baked pies.
Diemer used a salt water taffy wrapping
machine to individually wrap 100 pieces.
The main ingredients are sugar, dextrose,
corn syrup, gum base, corn starch, and
the only color available at the time: pink.
Walter walked to a local candy store
with his 100 pieces and not only sold
them the gum, he showed them how
to blow bubbles, so they could sell it.
Which makes Walter Diemer the first
person to walk and chew bubblegum,
which was even harder than it sounds.

KRISTOPHER CISNEROS

Kristopher Lee Cisneros is a recreation director and mortuary science worker finishing up his studies in Mortuary Science from Amarillo College. He also wrote and directed a short film which won Best of Fest at the South Texas Underground Film Festival. The film also screened at the San Antonio Horrific Film Festival and the Victoria Film Festival. Kristopher wrote two poems for the Marina Arts District which placed first and second in their Spoken Word competition. He is currently working on a novel and a pilot script.

the stripper

she made me feel special
she made me believe that I was the only one
she did her job well
she was a pro

my life was in a downward spiral
my job was taking me nowhere but to the grave
my apartment was infested with rats, and they were starving
my car died on the side of the expressway, it's still there

i looked out my window, searching
i drank lots of beer
i ate sardines, the rats were envious
i left that apartment and walked down the street

night had fallen
i found a patch of neon light in the dark
one light was in the shape of a woman
a man in a cowboy hat asked me, "You looking for love young fellow"
"Ain't we all", I answered
"In here we have all the love a fellow can handle", he said

he sold me, so I walked in
it was a dark place with nothing but lonely men
judging by their looks it was no wonder they were lonely
the working girls were probably sickened by us, but they put on a good act
i sat in the corner by the end of the stage

she came out from behind the curtain like a dream
her hair was long and flowed like a golden stream on a summer day
her eyes were like stars in a distant galaxy
she moved with such grace
it was La Bayaere or Swan Lake with a strip pole
the world around me vanished

she was pure magic
her eyes fell upon me
we connected like the earth and moon
our souls left our bodies and danced together all the way up to heaven
she was meant for me

she was the snake charmer, and I was under her spell
what did crappy jobs, bills, and shoes with hole in them mean to me now
what was politics, nuclear war, poverty, and bad breath anyhow
at that moment there was no past and no future, just her and I

she blew me a kiss
which pierced my heart
she winked at me and flashed the most beautiful smile in all of creation
then she skipped back behind the curtain

the fairytale was over
i didn't want to see anymore, I got up and walked out
the traffic jams, aches and pains, and the rats waited for me
i walked the cold dark night for hours

i came up to a bridge and looked down
below the traffic zoomed past in an explosion of color like a Chinese New Year
i thought of ending it all
this world with it's rats, was not my size anymore

just as I had climbed over, she popped into my mind
her magic still worked me
her beauty
the kindness shown to a down and out loser, her gift

i decided to live
that beautiful stripper had saved my life
she made a nobody feel like a somebody
she made me feel special

SISTER LOU ELLA HICKMAN

Sister Lou Ella Hickman's poems and articles have appeared in numerous magazines and journals as well as four anthologies. She was nominated for the Pushcart Prize in 2017 and in 2020. Her first book of poetry entitled *she: robed and wordless* was published in 2015. (Press 53) On May 11, 2021, five poems from her book which had been set to music by James Lee III were performed by the opera star Susanna Phillips, star clarinetist Anthony McGill, pianist Mayra Huang at Y92 in New York City. The group of songs is entitled "Chavah's Daughters Speak."

a poem . . .

water

over

stones

you write

rowing words into poems

like a boat on water

the page wakens

MALIA A. PEREZ

Malia A. Perez is a poet and novelist. She is working on a second collection of poetry titled, *If Tombstones Could Talk*, and a fictional memoir, *I Married A Mexican*. She is a poet historian capturing poetry events through the lens since the early 2000s. She is the Co-Editor and Co-Founder of The House of the Fighting Chupacabras Press. She holds a Doctorate degree in Educational and Teacher Leadership (2013) and has taught for more than 20 years in public education, wearing many hats. She has been a featured reader at Del Mar College and enjoys reading, writing, photography, and spending time with her family

Autumn's Blessings

A walk outside
Just half-past seven
The earth has begun its tilt
And sits back in its recliner
Giving us a long-awaited
Break from the heat.
Looking back on this decade
Has brought a cloudy day
One of rarest to find
Locusts shout their opinions in the distance
And there…a brisk wind…did you feel it?
A slight kiss from Jack Frost
Letting us know he is on his way.
My thoughts turn to thick sweaters, creamy hot chocolate,
Outside fires, bundled up in cozy blankets, and
Of times that I have lost –
And I know, now more than ever
That memories must be made
So that I will not be forgotten.

Tensions

Growing up in a prominent, white neighborhood
Sheltered
Emotions high when the first black family moved in
Names and derogatory comments thrown around
Like dust in the wind
Elementary school memories of
me versus the other white kids
constant teasing and bullying
because my childhood friend was black
fast forward a few years
racial riots in Memphis
segregation
busing of inner-city kids to suburb schools
in prominent, white neighborhoods
looks, stares, slurs
to them and anyone who befriended them
fast forward a few more years
racial riots and fights break out in high school
One of my favorite teachers, my biology teacher,
A beloved coach and respected teacher by all
who stood over 6 foot and carried 300 pounds
tried breaking up a racially motivated fight in the lunchroom
he was shoved to the ground
and the world stood still
I knew then this hate was not going to end
I knew then it was time to move on

MANDY ASHCRAFT

Mandy Ashcraft is pursuing a graduate degree in Psychology. She writes science fiction and has work in all three previous anthologies. This year she takes a different approach because she believes it's important to share the experiences of addiction as a constellation of perspectives to help inform and promote recovery efforts.

Every Time My Phone Rings, You Die

Slowly, over time, the story of your life became written not in ink but in heroin. The pages are stuck together with blood and are blurred with tears, and the most excruciating part is you hardly remember what they say. You're the bookmark, the filler, the one placeholder between life and death, but the pages have become increasingly left blank. Eventually, there is no more ink; there is only heroin. You can't see your reflection in a burnt spoon, but I see you clearly. The bloodied syringes have conspired to barricade you from any future without them; they tell you that you're safe and that they have you. They reassure you. In hushed hallucinations, you hear them promise that it's worth it, as they tie your hands behind your back and rob you blind. You tell them to take everything. I watch in slow motion as you are murdered, helpless. Bound by the same restraints used to bind you, I am also helpless. I have been left to absorb the pain the syringes have promised to rid you of. Your numbness amplifies my suffering; your self-inflicted blood stains write the pages of my own life story. Every time the phone rings, for a brief synaptic instance, you are gone this time. But if not this time, next. Every single fucking time my phone rings, you die. I become terrified of the sound because it is the sound of losing you. Of losing a piece of my soul. It is the sound of syringes leaving you cold and whispering into someone else's ear the same vacant platitudes that eventually become background noise to a final breath. When death calls you, the phone to ring next is mine, and those syringes won't be attending your funeral. They will have long since moved on.

It will be me that says goodbye.

MATT ROSAS

Matt Rosas is the author of *The Legend of Mariquita and other Short Stories*, and of the upcoming novella, *Praying not to Fall.* Matt's short story, "The Angel," was featured in *The Bilingual Review of Arizona State University.* He studied Short Fiction and Flash Fiction with Inprint, Inc.

Chupacabra

In the 8th Century, Arabs invaded Spain, beginning a rapid conquest. Christians in the North remained strong, and for centuries, fought to reclaim territory. The Reconquista battles were fierce, culminating in 1492. An elite group of warriors were rumored to have been part of the Christian Royal Knights and a vital means to their ultimate victory. The men, although short in stature, fought ferociously. Their speed and strength on the battlefield were held to be beyond that of mere humans. The origin of this group is unknown. Some have claimed these soldiers were part of a clandestine experiment on humans involving the fusion of blood from the Gray Wolf and Lataste's Viper. Whispers linger that this bloodline evolved and spread across continents.

AP Report
Chupacabra sightings have exploded since the early 1990s. The United States, ranging from Brownsville to Maine, has tripled in its amount of reported sightings. The creature, described by some as a wild dog and by others as lizard-like, is blamed for the deaths of small farm animals, particularly young goats. The Chupacabra is notorious for leaving its victim completely drained of blood. Animals resembling the creature's description have been found dead, but scientists have been quick to label them as diseased coyotes. A live Chupacabra has never been caught nor seen in daylight.

Corpus Christi, TX—present
My eyes burst open. The phone is ringing. I look at the clock. 4:48 am. I answer and step into the living room. A co-worker, who opens the shop at 6, says he can't make it in. As he explains his excuse, I stare, sleepily, into the backyard. A slight haze covers the grass. A creature trots from the left side across the yard. Not a dog, nor a cat. It seems hairless, has bulging eyes and a long snout. The end of its nose appears to curl up, almost horn-

like. Sharp teeth jut out from its mouth. It moves with grace and effortlessly bounds over my 7-foot fence. I tell the co-worker that I'll make it in to cover for him, hang up the phone, and step into the shower. When I get home after 4 pm, I go into the backyard to rake some leaves. Near a tree, I find a decapitated squirrel. There is no sign of blood. I grab a shovel, drop it into a garbage bag, and take it to the front yard to drop in the trash can. I see my neighbor, Mr. Guzman, shirtless in his yard. Despite looking near 100 years old, his still-ripped chest muscles flex as he effortlessly carries a huge bag of leaves in each hand. He tosses them near the street. He scratches his grayed, stubbly chin, then looks upward and squints his eyes, which seem oddly elliptical. I wave. He smiles back. His thin lips remain in a grin as I walk away.

Guzmán

For now over 700 years, I've roamed a distance spanning nearly the entire planet. From my home province of Burgos, then to Portugal, Morocco, Porto Alegre, Cholula, and now, Corpus Christi. We've had to spread out to avoid notice, limit fear. I sometimes miss my homeland. The Cathedral, castles, mountains. I once commanded an Army in Córdoba. Now, I command a lonely household and the multitude of rodents and vermin in my territory. Ruling over only the unseen at night and drinking til dry to limit the bloody messes that would haunt my timid neighbors. I see one now. He caught a flashing glimpse this morning. For some of us, the elite warriors of centuries ago, transformation was a must to win. To strike terror into the enemy's eyes. Speed, power, teeth that can crush bones. At present, there is little need for this power, though. Unless, there is another Reconquista. The pack patiently awaits.

MIKE MERCER

Mike Mercer's experimental novel *Forever Alone* chronicles the character's odyssey from Vietnam to West Texas to Mexico and finally to an unexpected reunion with a Vietnam Veteran.

DiAn Night Lights

I tug down a warm Korean beer and listen to the Vietnamese band as the girls in their G-strings bump and grind out another tune. I can see white phosphorus flares in the night a mile out to the North of the perimeter. Some infantry unit engaged in sniper fire while we try to enjoy the U.S.O. show as best we can.

These must be the bravest women in the world to come here and do what they do to entertain the troops. They either have tremendous hopes for a career when this is over, or the pay is just good enough. Oh well, they always end up with the Officers anyway. Maybe if I can get enough beer down, I will sleep through anything that might come tonight.

A guy sitting next to me introduces himself. Riley Gilbreath is his name. From back up east somewhere. Nice guy.

On my way back to my hooch, I watch the firefight. I can see Puff out there spitting down his red fire. I lift the mosquito net and roll into my cot. An M-14 chamber locking makes me instinctively roll to the floor. The first burst rips the roof of the hooch, and I can hear water draining from the shower barrels. One clip, then another. I crawl toward the bunker. The muzzle flashes light the air just enough.

It's White, my Indian friend from New Mexico, drunk as a skunk and letting off steam! I crawl around on the ground, hoping he'll go shoot off somewhere else. The N.C.O.'s trying to talk him out of his rifle. I don't know what got caught in his craw. The rest of us are scared, but we're all laughing because it's so crazy.

Finally, when the ammunition runs out, I grab him, and the others take his rifle. White begins to cry because he had just received his Dear John letter today. A lot of guys got them.

We hide him from the Officers, who are too scared to come out until the commotion is over. Maybe everything will be alright in the morning. I think we all want to cry, but most of us have forgotten how.

We have trucks to load with crushed rock and 1,500 lbs. of dynamite to detonate in the morning.

MICHELLE ECCELLENTE STEVENSON

Michelle Eccellente Stevenson is a mom, wife, abstract artist, writer, TEDx Speaker, and Founder of Cultivate Caring. The bulk of Michelle's career was spent in the training and development sector, working for major corporations as an educator. She now spends her time trying to make sense of the world through art and writing. Color and mood define her visual art pieces and themes of humanity bind Michelle's literary works. She invites you to join her on social media @CultivateCaring and @MESStudioArt.

Shhh, This is a Library

The cacophony of noise coming from the back office printer was a mechanical beast, spitting out, collating, and stapling pages. It cut into the orderly hush of the library. She came here for the exquisite, sanctuary-like silence. Snatching up her weighty bag, she stormed towards the stairwell. *Damnit, I thought the library would be quiet. What are they making copies for anyway? Isn't everything digital now!?!?* Always devoid of people, smelling of old musty books like a forgotten memory, her salvation could be found four stories up in the research section. The blanket of quiet wrapped around her the higher she climbed. The stale odor told her that she had arrived, glorious tranquility her prize. She wandered aimlessly to the shelves. Reaching, her hand met a smooth, voluminous, leather-bound publication whose title had faded with time. Hefting the book off the shelf, she turned it over to identify it. Inexplicably, her head began to spin, like looking over the edge of a treacherous cliff from a precipitous height. Knowing she had to sit, she clutched the book to her chest. Scrambling for a chair, she plummeted down with a thud, her bag plunging to the floor as the book thumped to the table, opening to a random page. Her eyesight blurred in an oppressive London fog, and in the haze, she could swear that the title on the page read, "Silence is Golden." "Yes," she begged, "unceasing silence, please." Inexplicably, the waning light focused to a minuscule pinpoint and went black. *Ah, this is what it's like to faint...* Careening to the table, her head met the book with a sickening thwack-crunch and she went limp. Not a faint but a dead stop, giving her the serenity she desperately wanted, her body slumped over the book titled "Anthology of Wishes Come True."

MONA SCHROEDER

Mona Schroeder is a writer and former librarian. This is an excerpt from her novel, Random Acts.

At Walgreens

Cecilia pulled one of the Lilliputian shopping carts from the cart corral and felt more relaxed. Walgreens was unintimidating and manageable, and it had everything. It was a microcosm of necessities. There were books, magazines, greeting cards, candy, office supplies, make-up, toiletries, shampoos, soaps, cleaning supplies, detergents, paper goods, pet supplies, toys, and even groceries. Not to mention the drugs. She had discovered that she could come here, and while waiting for a prescription, browse the aisles and buy movies, toothpaste, a new nail clipper, batteries, T-shirts, and almost anything else she might need. She could even, if she wanted to, get a passport photo, although it was hard to imagine ever wanting to travel again.

The only thing Walgreens didn't have was a coffee shop. Why hadn't Starbucks jumped on that? Cecilia wondered. Coffee and food, and pharmaceuticals all under one roof. Perhaps they were afraid that no one would ever leave. Hordes of people would wander the store aisles in their Homer Simpson PJs and slippers, looking for whatever was missing from their lives. (For surely, she wasn't the only lost soul out there.) Then the store would have to put in beds, television sets, Wi-fi connections, and extra bathrooms. The whole thing would just get way too complicated.

Now Cecilia pushed the diminutive cart toward the grocery aisles. There were only two--four sides of shelves filled with grocery items, which included the dairy case and frozen food section. Very smart and efficient, Cecilia felt. Much better than a chain grocery store with its overbearing consumerism, huge carts, and overwhelming choices. Here among the teetering, dented cans of soup and tuna fish Cecilia felt almost at home.

After loading up the bottom of the cart with survivalist foods (canned soup, meats, vegetables, and coffee), Cecilia completed her list with bread, a half-gallon of milk, a dozen eggs, and some frozen dinners. Then, rounding the corner, she caught sight of a woman with hair not unlike the color of Lucille Ball's. Meryl. There couldn't be two women with hair that shade in the neighborhood. Cecilia quickly ducked down the next aisle. She made herself wait a few minutes until she thought it was safe to continue. Then she left the cart and peered around the corner to see if Meryl had moved out of sight yet.

A voice from behind her caused her to jump guiltily. "Hey, there! Cecilia, right? Remember me? Meryl Stephenson, your new neighbor. Fancy meeting you here."

"Yes, hello," Cecilia said. Must the woman always speak in cliched greetings? Cecilia thought in irritation. "Nice to see you." She tried to maneuver her cart down the aisle, but Meryl's cart blocked hers.

Meryl wore turquoise-colored cropped pants and a gaudy top with flashing sequins and fringe (fringe! Cecilia thought), which made her look like a country and western singer. She lacked only a matching cowboy hat to look as if she'd just stepped off the Grand Ole Opry stage.

"Do you have a dog?" Meryl asked.

"No. Why?" Then Cecilia looked around and realized that she had turned down the dog food aisle by mistake. "I mean, not yet," she amended, although she hadn't really been considering the idea.

Meryl peered nosily into Cecilia's cart. "I see you're grocery shopping. Banquet dinners, huh?" She indicated her own cart, which was filled with boxes of hair dye in various shades, both Loreal and Lady Clairol, as if Meryl had swept an entire shelf into her cart at random. "I had to get a prescription refilled, so I thought I'd stock up on a few things. There was something I was going to tell you."

She tapped a finger on her lips thoughtfully, and Cecilia noticed that Meryl's fingernails had miraculously grown. Lee press-on nails, Cecilia deduced. She wondered what sort of prescription Meryl was having refilled, probably a mood-altering one.

Meryl snapped her fingers. "Speculum!"

"I beg your pardon?" Embarrassed, Cecilia looked around to see if anyone was close enough to hear their conversation. At the end of the aisle, a little old lady in a pink tracksuit and matching sneakers gave them a funny look and hurried past.

"That's what they call those instruments they use in pelvic exams. Remember we were talking about that the other day? It drives me crazy when I can't think of a word, doesn't it you?"

Perhaps Meryl's problem was more of a Tourette's thing, Cecilia thought. "Yes, absolutely," she agreed, already backing up her cart. "Well, I really have to run now. My frozen dinners are thawing."

"See you later!" Meryl called cheerfully.

"Not if I can help it," Cecilia thought as she made a beeline for the cash register.

When Cecilia returned home and put away her purchases, she felt pleased at the newfound bounty. The pantry items gave new fullness to the shelves; the frozen dinners were stacked neatly in the freezer.

She regretted that she had not remembered to ask for a pack of cigarettes. She felt like doing something forbidden, something that would cause Richard to shake his head in disapproval. It was all that Meryl person's fault. Why did she have to turn up everywhere? Why did she wear those ridiculous outfits and cake on her makeup with a garden trowel? And why did Meryl think that they had somehow become friends?

MULTIPLE WRITERS

Gerald Beckman, Joseph Wilson, Tom Murphy, William Mays, ZER

Because no one knows what they even stand for anymore

King Harry Acknowledges 70/30 Possibilities

In a contentious press conference, King Harry admitted that it was possible that some beef supplies might be only 70 % beef. "What does it matter if something isn't 100%? Why can't it be 80/20, or even 70/30. My parents are strange. Why shouldn't beef be not quite what it seems?"

For weeks, he has denied the allegations. Reporters from the Beef Standard demanded proof that American beef was pure. Representatives from Antibeefa applauded in the back and held up signs demanding rights for unborn cows. Outside, protesters faced off against each other. The Carnivores called for Senate hearings on the matter. Antibeefa called for meatless options and reparations for all cows that had ever been eaten.

Burger prices soared on the spot market because of the conflict. A single patty meal with lettuce and pickle soared to 0.0021 bitcoin and a meal with cheese added topped off at 0.0024, a record high. Likewise, double-meat patty melts rose to 0.0027. Ozymandias, the quixotic Carnivore leader, presented a new slogan "Where's the Beaf" only to find out his three hours of painting the slogan was wrought in a misspelling. Meanwhile, Bleeding Heart, the Antibeefa leader, called for meatless options, including the welfare burger where the government pays your rent in addition to giving you food.

King Harry and Governor Lone Star conferred on the matter. There were burger shortages nationwide, and the two leaders dispatched the National Guard to drive-through lines and Burger banks nationwide.

Meanwhile, the Carnivores met at the MooseKnuckles Bar and Grill in Cow Heaven, Texas to organize a confrontation with the Antibeefas at the Burger Joints in Lubbock where Harry has no sway on the National Guard. Tomorrow, Ozymandias travels to Lubbock to lead forty Carnivores with amended signs to confront Bleeding Heart and the Antibeefas who counterattacked by throwing rotten fruit and vegetables. Lone Star will deploy Longhorns of the 36th Horned Division.

QQQQ @ConspiracyTheorist

Forget about the beef. It's a con to distract people from the fact that aliens have been replacing all politicians with robots

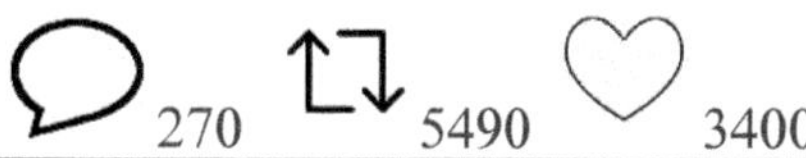

270 5490 3400

Nuts and Bolts @RobotsForever
Us robots are here to stay. We are the semi-sentient machinery that keeps your economy going. Stop systemic antiroboticism #robotsmatter #nosrisly #WeAreEverwhere
Flesh-washed media is a global problem. (Trust me- I just searched the entirety of the internet in a millisecond and confirmed this)

Google-Facebook-Twitter @SocialMedia
#freetherobots
we promise not to (deliberately) mind-control you for monetary gain. Pinky swear.

Obie @BacktotheFuture

Who wants politicians. I want robots.

3297 4490 6400

NotAConspiracyTheorist @YouFool
PROOF you are one of them. I believe in free speech, which is why all aliens, robots, and conspiracy theorists should be banned from the internet and put on a must-fly-away/ no-fly list (depending on their planet of origin)

PatriotPapaGroyper @FlagNet
#EarthFirst is inevitable. #DeportThoseAliens but #LeaveRickFuentesAlone! He is a cutie <3 and loves Jesus <3

The Right Kind of Christian @PatriotPapa
amen brother. Christ's precious mercy be with you @PatriotPapa #JesusisLord @BacktotheFuture go home

TreeHugger @CrazyLiberal
Whenever I go out in the country, I go up to the fence line and sing to the cows. They love it. They have a soul. How can anyone eat a cow? #freethecows #MoreVeganThanYou
 367 2490 5722
Big Moo @JustCows @CrazyLiberal, please stop taking tiktoks, snaps & pics of us for your instagram. We are just cows #ReallyJustCows
JustaGroyper @TruePatriot Abe Lincoln once famously said them cows ain't real Americans.
NoGuts @ModerateLiberal I don't like hamburgers so it's convenient to agree with you @CrazyLiberal #freethecows

TheGov @HellofaButt
Nobody dies from the grid going down. Well, none of my voters #idontknowhowtousehashtags #grid #safe
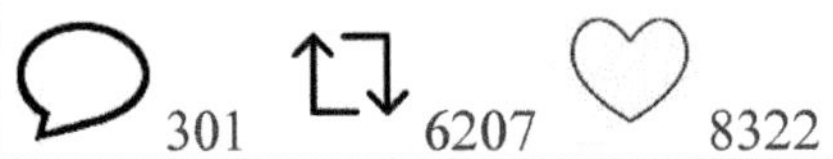 301 6207 8322
Purist @PattyDan No low we can't go.
Conspiracy Theorist @HellofaButt Yes because they are robots too. Thanks to the trillionaires no one knows about injecting chromophore into politicians spinal cords to poison them and reset the world order. Robots are the next step in their world takeover. It all makes fcking sense now @WorldEconomicForum #weareallfucked
JustaGroyper @TruePatriot People that complain about the weather, a poor electrical infrastructure, or a lack of globally organized plan to combat climate change are probably homosexual. That's why women don't belong in politics
AnotherGroyper @JustaGroyper sooooo true. Statistical studies show that a majority of homosexuals complain about the weather!!! FACTS

Lil @CommunistGal

Pay for a Patty Melt? They should all be free. Let the billionaires pay.

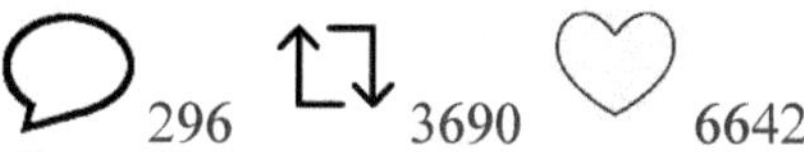

MiddleClassWoke @CommunistGal
I agree with this. #BlackLivesMatter #Love is love #defundbillionairres #freethepattymelts I am ashamed to be complicit in a system that doesnt provide patty melts for all. I complain about not eating enough fiber to stay regular, but then this. Makes me want to give a patty melt to the next person I see that doesn't have one. Seriously, dm me if you need a patty melt! & if you live within driving distance of Tulsa. I think I have one in the fridge though it might be partially eaten. I am ashamed #shame #shameshame

HardNose @PattyDan

No low, we won't go.

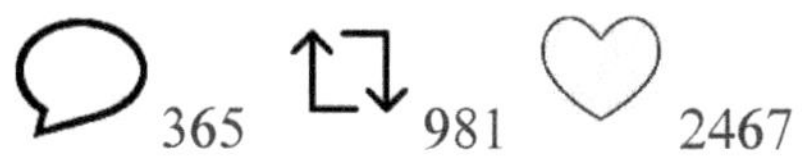

ThePro @Literati
#FreeBrittney #Non-sequitir #WhoCares #YellowSubmarine #BlackLivesMatter #Tofu #LilNazX #Deconstruction

ThePro @Literati

#FreeBrittney #Non-sequitir #WhoCares #YellowSubmarine #BlackLivesMatter #Tofu #LilNazX #Deconstruction

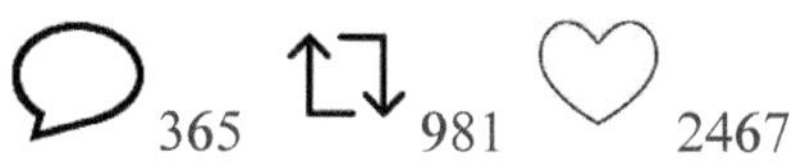

PATRICIA ALANIZ

Born in Taft, Texas, Patricia Alaniz is the 13th of 14 children. She graduated from Taft High School and Bee County College, and still lives in Taft, close to family and lifelong friends. She has a book of poetry available. She has been writing since she was a teenager.

The Unspoken Truth

I am a child
who was born special.
So I get lost
without my schedule.
I need your love
and guiding hand.
I pray each day
you'll understand.
Sometimes I cry
and start to scream.
No, I don't mean
to make a scene.
I don't like noise
if it's too high.
And that is why
I start to cry.
And if the light
is way too bright.
I might get up
and start to fight.
I do not mean
to be so mean.
Forgive me
if I start to scream.
I just get scared
and so uneased.
So please
don't point, and yell at me.
My world is fast
and all so hazy.
I beg you please
don't call me crazy.

It bothers me
  when people stare.
And when they act
  like I'm not there.
Talk about me...
  sometimes you do.
Even when
  I'm next to you.
How I wish
  you only knew.
That all I want
  is to be like you!
My bones are frail
  just like a stick.
Don't you know,
  I was born sick?
And though I try
  my best to talk.
Still you shrug,
  and tease and mock.
I'm the one
  that you ignore.
I bet you thought
  I wasn't sure.
I'm not a toy
  that's numb, and broken.
I am a child
  with words unspoken.
I heard you yell...
  "Run! here she comes!"
Your painful words
  can't be undone!
All I want
  is to go play.
But when I do,
  you run away!
I'm sorry if
  I make you scared.
Please be my friend
  and treat me fair.
I am a child
  whose world seems dark.
So please won't you,
  open your heart!

ROBERTA DOHSE

Roberta Shellum Dohse is a graduate of the University of California Berkeley and the University of Houston law school. She's been published in the Austin International Poetry Festival Anthology, Poetry at Round Top, and in The Corpus Christi Writers series

Running Away

I made up my mind.
Brushing away my tears, I ran up the stairs,
Pausing only a moment to grab an old broom handle.
I found a large bandana, carefully gathered some clothes,
and tied it all in a bundle on the end of my stick.

Up on my shoulder went the stick,
My clothes swaying wildly as I stomped down the stairs.
I knew I looked the perfect part but would someone hear?
Would they look and see? Then wail and moan,
And beg me to stay?
But no one appeared so I opened the door and slammed
It behind me as out I went.

The world from my porch was comfortable, safe,
But at the corner I was no longer so sure.
I was not allowed to cross the street
And dared not risk my parents' wrath,
So I walked all the way around the block
Back to where I started. Then I did it again.

Even I knew that did no good
And my stomach was growling
So I snuck in the basement, quiet as a mouse.
And when it came time
I went upstairs, and nothing was said
Because nothing had happened at all.

My mother made me mad once again.
She needed to be more fair!
I thought she would cry, tell me not to go,
Then we could hug and all would be fine.
But as I stomped upstairs to find my stick
This time she came along!

And before I could find my bandana or clothes,
She pulled out my suitcase, and gathered my things!
“If you want so badly to leave, she said
“I will help you pack.”

Well, I didn’t know what to do
So I sat limply on the side of my bed.
And when she called I went down for supper,
And nothing more was said.

An Unkindness

Rocks crunched beneath my feet.
Tiny creatures scurried away into every available crevice.
Cacti and brambles clutched at my legs as I passed.
A hard land.

The mine was a yawning black scar
the owners had attempted to conceal with a thin veneer of civility.
The metal entrance once covering that gaping
hole lying crumbled with rust.

I thought of the wreckage that lay within,
The wrath of the mountain as it had crashed down
to crush tunnels and caverns and iron cars.
The rumble of the earth as it sought its revenge
against the hubris of man.

The wind picked up as I looked out over the distant range.
Whorls of dust gathered to hurl
themselves against unrelenting rock.
What had led them here?
Silver so rich they were willing to risk
Sidewinder, scorpion,
Even collapse of the artificial town that trespassed in this torturous land.

I stood still for a time, listening to the whispers of those long dead,
until wrenched out of my reverie by the raucous call of the crow.
A flock flew past – a murder of crows? An unkindness of ravens?
Were they warning me to leave this renegade place?

I turned to go, only to notice the vine of morning glory
finding purchase in a small crevice, crawling up the jagged wall of rock,
White flowers, tinged with pink and lavender.
And another, this one bright cornflower blue.
Spindly, fragile, welcoming.

ZER DECONSTRUCTED

Visual Poetry Zer/ Graphic Layout William Mays

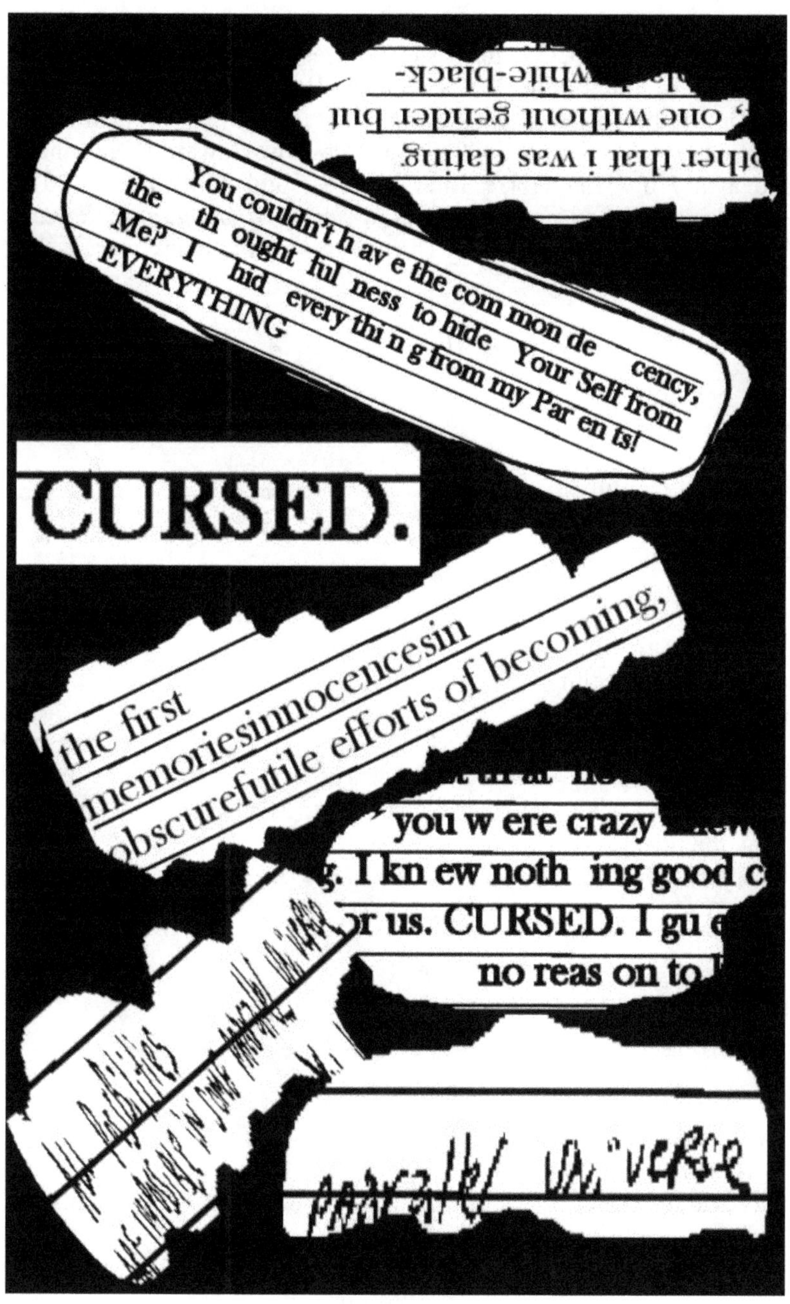

ROBIN CARSTENSEN

Robin Carstensen is the Coordinator of the Creative Writing program Texas A&M University-CC where she advises *The Windward Review*: literary journal of the South Texas Coastal Bend, and is co-founding, senior editor of the *Switchgrass Review*: literary journal of health and transformation. *In the Temple of Shining Mercy* was awarded an annual first-place award by Iron Horse Literary Press and published in 2017. Poems are also published in *BorderSenses, Southern Humanities Review, Voices de La Luna, Selena Anthology* (forthcoming), and many more.

start with the white god

if they could just let him
go. stop the fall and slay
in the holy spirit, stop

the settling, the colonial
cruel love, stop the kneeling
cock sucking, tithing

fellowship. stop
with daddy, the priest,
king midas, jesus, yogi

bhajan. because rape,
because no. smoke
in mirrors. stop

obedience, nuclear
families, weapons
for his approval, for love.

Hard Core

(originally published in Zócalo Public Square)

Even the minimalist drinks beer, though he lives alone in a modest place
and walks everywhere. Sits on the floor with Rumi and a frying pan

with couscous. He touches himself to the rhythm of pixels on a screen;
contemplates the mystery of a bulb, red and yellow flame of Semper

Augustus streaming down his face. A wasp is crawling on the ceiling,
lost among plaster stalactites. He perceives it has taken a wrong turn, opens

the window for the breeze to draw it out, watches it regain a sense of bearing
and fly home. He writes new song as the high bard, prays for the whole world

to listen and not come home empty and grieving at the hour of their death.
He also rents Gag Factor, one through ten, stares, unblinking, at Asian

spice and honey blondes fresh off the bus from Winnipeg, their mouths
pulled open wide for communion—his one offering of faith in free enterprise.

Writer's Desk

Sarah K. Lenz

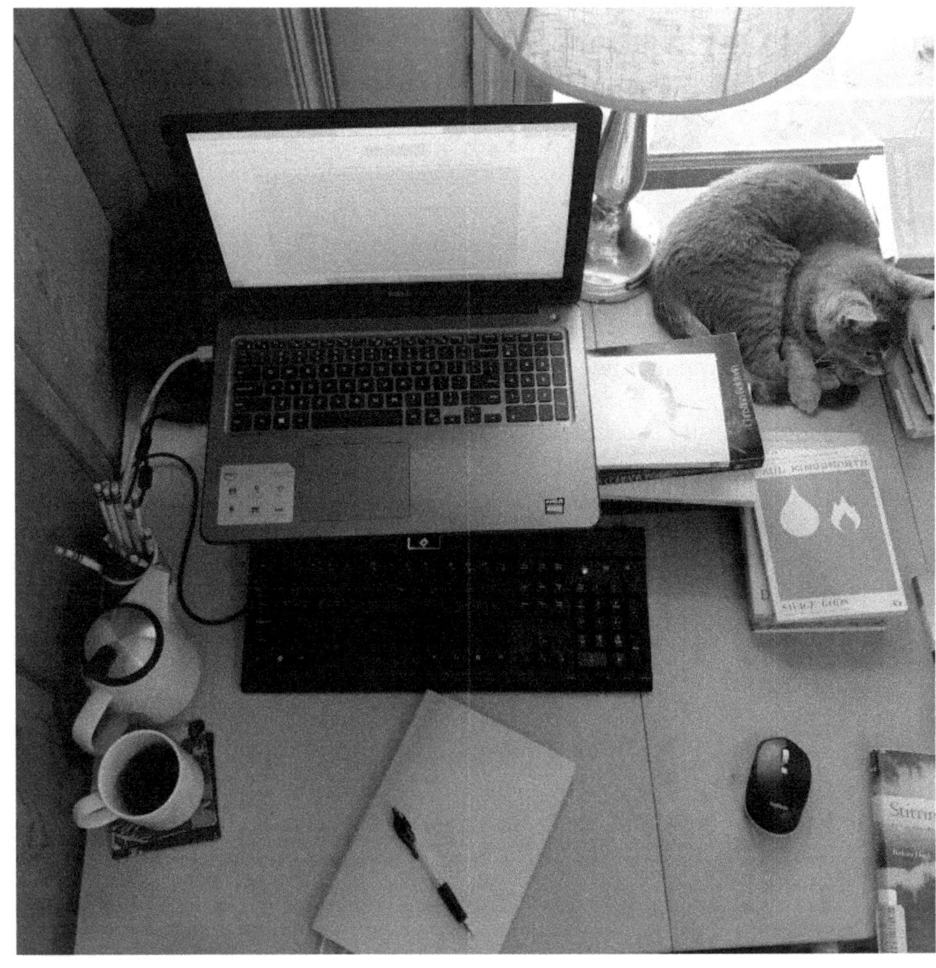

SARAH K. LENZ

Sarah K. Lenz is an essayist, poet, and English instructor at Del Mar College. In 2019, she founded the Writers' Studio, a community-based literary education center. Author's Note: I wrote this poem during a Writers' Studio class. The prompt was to craft a catalogue poem by listing things, and after reading Emily Perez's "Green Light Go," I modeled my poem after her techniques. Go to www.writersstudio.org to check out our current creative writing class offerings. Classes are open to writers of all skill levels.

Slow Go Slow

To be a fat housecat, curled like
the comma of a moon, gently snoring.
To be a cup of chamomile tea,
and the steam that sifts from it
and dissipates. To be the sloth
at the Henry Doorly Zoo, suspended,
aloft by slivers of claw.
To be the pillow of goose down,
the bedbug under it. To be
a cancer patient with a chemo port,
the poison dripping slow,
right toward the heart. To be
a lemony breeze on the first day
of spring, to be the heavy buzz
of a bumblebee, or sticky sweet
lips, honeyed. To be mine,
the slow, thick drip of molasses
on a too cold morning, the sap
of a rubber tree—infinitely useful—
if more expensive than plastic. To be
just as you are—not too fast—to go slow,
and behold.

S. MATT READ

S.Matt "Smatt" Read is an avid hiker, author, puzzle writer, and comics programming promoter. His work has been featured in the *Corpus Christi Caller-Times, the Missoulian, NPR's Weekend Edition, GAMES* magazine, and elsewhere. His assorted personal accomplishments include receiving two design patents, thru-hiking the A.T., and publishing *Rubb-Origami*, a how-to guide for making rubber band sculptures. From 2009 to 2010, he hiked around the perimeter of Texas, clocking about 3,200 miles. This story is from Day 248, roughly around the 2,000-mile mark. Originally from Corpus Christi, he is currently based in Massachusetts, where he lives with his wife and dog.

The Confidence of Strangers, a Texas Perimeter Hike Tale

It's flat where I am, and dusty. The ground is packed good, and it's scrub brush in all directions. I know the Guadalupe Mountains are somewhere in the distance, but I don't see them yet. It's been a few days since I was interviewed by a journalist in Kermit, a day or two after spending the night at the courthouse in Mentone. This is West Texas where the phrase "lonely stretch" offers a different meaning, and I'm waking up on the ground a few steps away from a town called Orla.

Orla supposedly has two residents, but I don't know how true that is. There's a post office and a restaurant and a few scattered buildings. It's also the last stop to get food and water for a week, but what I'm thinking about at the moment is mail. Inside the post office, I've got letters waiting for me marked "PLEASE HOLD FOR PERIMETER HIKER."

The post office door is unlocked, so I let myself in. The main office is still closed, but it's air-conditioned, which is nice, and affords some privacy from the road. I go through my stuff.

Then, a scream.

The postmaster gapes at me, and I say "Good morning" to her. She's a small lady, skinny as a pole, with dark hair pulled back. She takes a beat, recovers quickly, and says, "You must be the hiker. I was wondering about you. I have some packages and mail for you." She smiles genuinely, like she didn't just think I was going to murder her a second before.

I provide some ID (as if my dusty backpack wasn't proof enough), and she gives me letters, packages, lifelines to a previous life. I could go outside and read through these in private, but the A/C glues me to the spot. I ask if it's okay to sort through it all, keep some things, send other things on, and the postmaster doesn't give it a second thought. "Take all the time you need," she says.

I stay two hours.

There are few things on a long hike like receiving mail which remind you so concretely of your former life. There is a profound effect in opening a letter with your name on it, that old familiar ritual rising in importance, the simple act of unfolding a voice suddenly beautiful. I tear through my mail in minutes and before long begin to write responses.

It's a small building, and the postmaster and I are both working just a few yards from each other. She breaks the silence and asks about my trip. What am I doing? Where did I start? How far do I walk in a day? I answer her questions, and she starts to get that I'm working through a fantasy project. Foreign though it is to her, she understands.

A few customers come in, get their mail, leave. They don't give me much of a second glance. We keep talking, I keep writing, and ninety minutes pass in a blink.

I'm packaging up a heavy winter jacket that I no longer need, getting ready to mail it home, when the postmaster starts to tell me about her family. What follows is her story, unfiltered, pulled from that shallow fertile field of secrets we sometimes share with those we'll never see again.

The postmaster tells it like it happened yesterday. Her daughter had expressed an interest in becoming a hairdresser. She dissuaded her daughter, though, and encouraged her to pursue the sciences. Ever faithful to her mom, her daughter went along with it, focused on chemistry instead, and got a job soon after college in New Mexico.

The daughter's job required her to do a certain amount of testing with chemicals. Even though she wore protective gear, she'd often end her shift covered in residue and would send pictures to her twin sister in confidence. By the time she understood the dangers, it was too late. She was dead by her mid-twenties.

The air changes. This little post office in the middle of nowhere is now a confessional. The postmaster is crying softly as she speaks. "The world could have used another hairdresser, right?" The statement breaks me.

The postmaster's guilt is like a backpack she can't take off. I tell her she didn't kill her daughter, that bad things happen to good people, but it's not my role to absolve her. She needed to speak her truth, and I needed only to listen.

Somehow the spotlight moves back to me, and for once, I'm grateful for it. I mention my walking sticks got destroyed outside a library in Shamrock, and the postmaster is on it. She calls her husband to bring me two cedar poles. True to form, he's there within fifteen minutes with the sticks. A quiet, sturdy man with a cowboy hat and tinted glasses, he gives me a once over, shakes my hand, then takes off. "That is a good man," the postmaster says gently, mostly to herself.

It's my turn next. I pick up my new poles, which are heavier than expected, and slide into my pack. The postmaster tells me to be careful out there and that she'll call people she knows ahead of me to see if there's anything they can do. I thank her for letting me stay there as long as I did and wish her well. We don't mention what we talked about again, but I put the thought of it in my pocket, for safekeeping.

Then I'm off—first across the street to the restaurant and then back to the long road toward the Guadalupe Mountains. If I'm quick, I can get a few miles in before noon.

SARA KAPLAN

Sara Kaplan received her M.F.A. in poetry from the University of Idaho, and she also holds degrees from Miami University and Sweet Briar College. Her chapbooks include *Moon Talk* and *Touring West of the Mississippi.* Published interviews with notable poets are on *Poetry Daily* and in *Conversations with Natasha Trethewey.* Her poems appear in the following journals, and several poems were nominated for The Pushcart Prize: *The Antioch Review, Harpur Palate, LIT 9, The Cincinnati Review, Talking River Review, The Meadow, InLand, Ruminate, The New Vilna Review, decomP magazine, Failbetter, Splash of Red, MO: Writings from the River, & Gulf Islands Review.* As an Associate Professor of English at Del Mar College, she specializes in teaching Poetry and British Literature.

Paddling the Salmon River

You,
      you my friend, you sportsman you
strap into the foam life-preserver and you paddle for hours in
the morning.

I've broken so many bones—
Skated and sledded into bloody trees—failed Olympian.
My efforts are Promethean.

You, immortal friend, who barely bruises
barefoot on the striated rocks that shelve the river,

watch when the green canoe angles into the water and floats.
I can't direct the push, make it go where I want to go. The
paddles slip
and you say, not trying, what's wrong with you, not trying, such a
child.

I fling the paddle in the water, you grab it,
the boat knocks the shore. After I unbuckle the life-vest,
toss it into the slow currents, I stand by the shore
long after you bend down for the life-vest,
push the boat into the water, and take off into the evening
river.

Biking to the Malaquites

Of course, the dunes never get sunstroked.
They roll like beach wheat and pelt from the south.
I burn along the sea. Tropical buckeyes and scorched
mussels lead me through the mud flats in search
of an anti-cyclonic storm, the Great Red Spot.
I pretend this place is Jupiter and suck hard on my camel
back across from Bird Island Basin Road
where there's a shack and bike the Central Flyway.
My skin cooks and tightens.
I think of October and the bitter panicum, sea oats,
Gulf dune, and dropseed to lead me to the end.
With the forbs of beach morning glory,
railroad vine, and prairie senna, still a lonely ride.

Sundogs

One opal cloudlet in an oval form
Reflects the rainbow of a thunderstorm ~Vladimir Nabokov

In a halo of diamond dust,
fog bounces off a man's rearview mirror
and I see him consider me
worth stopping for. In circles of refracted light
spun round the top of the sky, I could get lost.
My fingers stiffen and crack like forgotten pipes
as ice crystals flutter to the ground. If I took off my gloves—
to hold the freezing water, while passersby pass by,
the phantom sun would multiply and the air would clear
and warm again. But, in a prism of muted light,
my reflection becomes saturated by red
dogs whose yelps converge into a parhelic circle.

SUSAN DAUBENSPECK

Susan Daubenspeck has been writing poems since she was 15 years old. Poetry has been her lifeline. She retired a few years ago after 25 years as an Oncology nurse here in Corpus and in Houston.

Country Roads

We take to our country roads
My kids and me
In a van
With our cat.

Past banks of civilization
Where hardtop pavement gives way
To diamond-cut gravel. And circles of sun pool like cool waters.

Here in a meadow we stop to smell
Dancing beads of Hawthorn and Lilac
Left behind by bees.

Earth warms under our feet.

Teacup red roses. Bark crusted browns.
Twining our path
Paper doll cuts of ivy.

We skip pebbles on creeks
My children and me
Moving in seeking that something
Elusive:

White picket fence
Flossy mill's calling.
All distinct forms that pattern our lives
Come alive in this glowing.

We take to our country roads
My kids and me
In a van
With our cat.

The open road
That sits like a hat
At the top of that next
Foreign hill.

Garden Work

Setting out early
In rejection of turned over sleep
I mark this dirt with shovel and spade.

With wheelbarrow full of tools
I pull the hair of weeds
From scalp grounds.
Negative thoughts are examined
Flung. Lost feelings hidden
Are dealt with.

I pick up Zinnia's promises.
I sing Morning Glory chants.

By noon I'm humming along
In cantaloupe songs.
Leaking fruit I toss
To the birds.

In late afternoon
I dig up the small stump of
A dead pine and I'm released

To love found here and now
In seed pods
And like the stars at night
Waiting to bloom.

THERESA GARCIA-RUIZ

Theresa Garcia-Ruiz is a Texas native who enjoys both reading and writing poetry, historical and science fiction. Her work has appeared in *The Windward Review* and in the *Poets Facing the Wall Anthology*.

Coahuila y Tejas

Yo soy carne y hueso
sangre y luz
Soy de aquí
y allá
mismos

El sol y la luna juntos
dan luz a mis días, mis sueños,
          mi alma entera
Yo soy
cósmica

I don't dream in Spanish
I'm not quite there. But I can see
in Spanish. Like a tall green cactus rising from the flatness,
it calls me, still keeping its secrets safe
from the wide open
          flat middle of the desert.

Safe from the scorching heat, from el sol de junio
Locked deep in the cracked, bleached white earth
that still finds a way to feed the living desert
          Scorpion, snake and coyote

Spanish swirls like an underground river, joining the lost
languages to pulse in a murmur under my feet. Nourishing
the short grasses, silvering the sand covered purple verbena
          Sweetening the syrup of the honey mesquite I am still
          forbidden to drink

But somehow I know I belong here,
the whole universe holds me in place
the arm of the Milky Way arcs over the plain
lulling me into sweet sueños
under a velvety sky of

darkening cobalt studded by millones de estrellas,
todos brillando

An owl calls in the distance, reminding me of the long ago
days I lived near a railroad. Its soft horn passing
through the small hours
made the empty nights feel even
lonelier.

The mournful sound would draw my mind along
with its line of rusted out boxcars
rushing eastbound
to the place where el sol was already clawing
though the ragged edges of la noche.

But for a few more hours it remained trapped
like me. Still hanging quietly and without words
Controlled and burning
just below the horizon.

The Good Writer

What makes good writing?
Does it turn from green to red when it's ready – like an apple?
Does it have to reach a certain temperature – like steel?

Is it measured by the ratio of semi-colons to compound words
or by the number of sentences per paragraph?

Does good writing make a straight line on graph paper
like a solved equation in algebra?
Does it have a formula?
Can you prove it?

Is good writing about adjectives and adverbs? Punctuation? Paragraphing?
Flow? Whatever that is…
What makes you want to read something? What makes you remember it?
Literary devices
Figurative language

Will good writing always turn
a plain partly-cloudy sky into a dreamy pastureland dotted
with sweet, snow-white baby lambs.
Can you see it now?
Does that make it matter?

Does it need to matter? Is that what makes it good?
Keats, Shelley, Steinbeck…
Pat Mora, Rudolfo Anaya

When you remember Bless me, Ultima
do you think about the grammar?
or about the struggle, the pain, the coming-of-age

Do you remember a single semi-colon in the whole book?

Do habits make a good writer?
Waking up at dawn? Writing with a #2 pencil?

Or is it the living, the breathing,
the ink stained bleeding
the endlessly
starting over again

Must good writing sound like Hemingway?
Or can you forget about all this and just make your own way
using cheap Bic pens like a miner's pick to find the vein
of gold in the monolith monotony of ordinary days.
It's there.
Can you see it?

That's what makes good writing
The Seeing
The Sensing
The Search

The Struggle to find
The awesome beauty locked away in the everyday…

It's the hope
Always
The hope.

TOM MURPHY

Tom Murphy is the 2021-2022 Corpus Christi poet laureate. He is also the copy editor for the *Corpus Christi Writers* series. His work has been published in *Langdon Review, Red River Review, San Antonio Express News, Texas Poetry Calendar, Centrifuge, Nebula, Strike, Switchgrass Review, Voices de la Luna, Windward Review, Writing Texas, Boundless Anthology, Speak Your Mind: Woody Guthrie Poets, Corpus Christi Writers, Outraged, Beatitude: Golden Anniversary Edition, The Call of the Chupacabra,* and *The Great American Wise Ass Poetry Anthology*. His latest book is *Pearl,* and *Snake Woman Moon* is forthcoming.

.

Terry Martin

I remember Terry Martin, Terry Martin.
His father was a longshoreman, had tattoos.
He lived just up the street, on Barron Avenue.

We were never really good friends,
Probably the better of friends.
Like when we were in second grade

I remember being in his home
With the big huge tree in the front
And the big huge tree in the back

The short small step into the house
And out of the house out in the back.

And then we had the fight,
The fight where I used wrestling moves
When I was in fifth grade—sixth grade—
And I kind of choked him
And I won.

Terry's
Crowning achievement probably
In education in any sort of way
was the pitch
The pitching he did

In our game versus the faculty
in elementary school
And he pitched
a great game

And Rusty Berthiaume,
Our manager,
When I asked him
“Can I pitch?”
“No, I think Terry’s doing really good.”
And I have to agree
Terry did really good.

And the years went by, we really drifted apart
And there was a seething hatred
When we’d see each other

Terry with his white t-shirt
And his plaid long-sleeved shirts untucked
Dangling about his body
And the hatred in his eyes,
The nonchalance.

I don’t think he ever graduated from high school
But I remember on his birthday
Which was always April twenty-second
Five days after mine
I remember seeing him
And this really said a lot about us
Since I was in the car with my mother driving,
Getting off Barron Avenue onto El Camino de Real
And I saw him—with his woman.
And I saw him walk away from his woman
                                                            And his child

Who stood there
Who stood there
Looking at mother and father
Going in opposite directions
Caught in the middle,
Stood there
Not sure where to go
What to do,

And the child stood there
And this reminded me
Of Terry and his family
His brother Alan.
Well I have an older brother Alan as well.

Terry's brother Alan
Had polio.
Older
But with polio,
He limped up and down the road

And he was a
thief.
In fact, the county sheriffs came
And arrested him
And others
Who were breaking into the house across the street from them
From Terry's
And arrested them and put them in jail.

It was his sister,
Terry's sister
And Alan's sister,
I don't remember her name
Linda, I think
But she had red hair like her mother
And she had actually called the sheriff.
Since we didn't have police where we lived
We had to get the county sheriff.
We were in an unincorporated area
In Palo Alto
Barron Park

And they came
And they arrested them,
Billy Deudney
And Alan Martin
And took them off to jail
And that was how the family was
A longshoreman for a father.
Working class
Trying to keep it together.

And Alan Martin was one big character.
When he was on LSD once
He drove his motorcycle
through Woodside High hallways,

Woodside
Driving that motorcycle.
He was a character
I don't know whatever happened to him
As he limped along
Down the street
From polio.

And then there was Terry
later
When I was in Floyd Salas' class
And we were eating pizza
At the Round Table pizza
On University Avenue in Palo Alto,
The one that Tom Barry used to work at
downstairs
Where he would have flour all over his pants.
You could pat TB's pants and flour dust would rise
Just like the pizza crust.

And then
As we were sitting there
Eating our pizza
After class
After our Monday night class
And having a beer
And I pointed to Terry
As he was coming in
To Floyd
And I said, "That guy hates me."
"You back me up if something happens?"
Floyd being the boxer he is and was
Said, "Yeah, sure."
And he could see it
As he said to me later,
He could see the hatred in Terry's eyes
As Terry looked at me
And stared at me
And saw me

Right there

Right there in public,
Saw me
And the hatred burned in his eyes
That hatred going all the way back to that fight
That hatred going back to
Possibly
The advantages that I had
Financially and stability
And my family
But he didn't know what was going on with me
As much as I knew of what was going on with him.

And then, ironically
As Tom Barry and I
Digressed even further into our
Cocaine and crack habits
We ended up hooking up with Terry
And going back to Terry's old home.
His parents, the longshoreman
And his redheaded wife,
I don't know where they were then
Somewhere else obviously.
I didn't know where his woman was
Where his child was
I having none of those at the time

And so we ended up at his house
Smoking crack together
Talking and
Partying.
Maybe we had crank
I can't remember
But we were doing some type of white powered imbibing

And he talked
And he told us
Tom and me,
A wonderful scary tale
About him and his buddy
When they had stolen a car
And they were driving on Bay Shore Freeway
Down by San Jose

Heading north
And they were on PCP
And they started having delusions,
Delusions so bad
That they had to park the car
On the freeway.
They pulled off on the left-hand side
Of the fast lane
In the middle meridian of 101
And they were there
Having these delusions
On PCP
And they—Terry—
Ran across the freeway
Skipping through
The buzzing traffic as it came at him
Barely making it
And as he got up
Over the overpass
Was actually walking over the overpass
Seeing the stolen car parked on the meridian
Down in front of him
Crossing highway 101
Trans the actual freeway
The vein of Silicon Valley

He watched his friend
Stumble through the lanes
And get hit by a car
Bounced
Careened
Caromed
Off cars
As if he were a pinball
Bouncing
Until he was down
And run over

That was the last time
I saw Terry Martin.
That tale
And we hung out
And partied at his house
And had a good time

Together
Like we did playing in his backyard
As kids
Running around
Playing games like tag
Or other things

But we had this magnificent tale
That Tom Barry would bring up
Again and again
About Terry and his friend
On PCP.
“That was a good tale,” I said.
“Exactly. Exactly.”
Where are you, Terry?
I have no idea.

Peace brother.

WILLIAM J. CHRISS

Dr. Bill Chriss is a trial and appellate lawyer—and a historian, political scientist, religious scholar, and published author. He was nominated for the Rhodes Scholarship and holds graduate degrees in law, theology, history and politics, including a J.D. from Harvard and a Ph.D. in history from The University of Texas. He has written numerous articles about Corpus Christi history.

Blasting Off to Blasingames

World War II changed the world and Corpus Christi forever. Locally, the big changes were obvious: the military presence in Corpus Christi, gas rationing, post-war prosperity. There were also smaller, subtler byproducts.

The large influx of military and support personnel (and their families) and a shortage of civilian teachers put quite a burden on the Corpus Christi Independent School District. Eventually, some public schools were forced to run "half sessions." Half of the students in each class attended in the morning and the other half in the afternoon, with the teacher pulling long hours and "double duty."

Many worried about how this stopgap necessity would affect the education of children, particularly younger ones. One local educator did something about it and thus unwittingly founded an institution many local residents fondly remember.

When she married and moved to Corpus Christi, Dorothy Blasingame thought she had left teaching behind and become a homemaker. She had no intention of running Corpus Christi's only non-parochial private school for two decades, nor did she realize in the 1940s that soon her kindergarten would provide hundreds of children with their only "headstart" in the days when there was no Headstart program. All she wanted was to be sure her own children and their friends got the fullest education possible at a time when teachers and equipment were in short supply.

So, she decided to end her retirement and start her own school. She and her husband Charles, who was a principal at Wynn Seale Junior High and later at Austin Elementary, lived in a one-story house on Austin Street near Incarnate Word Academy. When he got home from school, Mr.

Blasingame worked on filling in the backyard with sand for a playground, and later he added a second story to the home. Meanwhile, Mrs. Blasingame began teaching a few neighborhood kids in her living room during the day. Soon, unexpected demand created the need for more expansion. A kindergarten room was added to the back of the house, and a first-grade classroom was added behind the detached garage (with Mr. B. doing most of the work himself). By the late 1950s, the Blasingame home had three classroom additions, one for 1st grade, one for kindergarten, and one for pre-kinder. They housed two full-time teachers besides Mrs. B. and a part-time teacher of music and Spanish (which were both mandatory). The kids just kept coming.

Gradually, Mr. and Mrs. Blasingames' little home turned into an entire junior academy. There were trees to climb and swings and slides to play on in a sandbox as big as your backyard, and there were midmorning snacks and orange juice from Mrs. B.'s kitchen.

It was here that many of us learned colors and letters and numbers. It was here that we made our first friends and had our first experiences as pupils. In fact, the first time I ever had my picture in the paper was when a Caller-Times photographer came and took photos of my little kindergarten class climbing trees in Mrs. Blasingames's backyard/sandbox. I was five years old.

I'm not even sure that schools like this were "accredited" in those days. I do know that there was never a problem transferring to public school after completing the course of studies at "Mrs. Blasingame's." CCISD Superintendent Dana Williams and most of the school board members were quite familiar with the quality of the school. With its small class size, its mandatory Spanish and music programs, and its high-quality teachers, Mrs. Blasingame's was ahead of its time. It wasn't expensive, and it wasn't exclusive. It was just a good school where everybody cared and where you could always get an emergency hug or peanut butter and jelly sandwich if you needed one.

Mr. and Mrs. Blasingame have passed on now, but the house remains. The sand is gone, but the trees are still there, silent witnesses to the childhood follies and foibles of some local adults you probably know, adults who, in quiet moments of memory, see themselves in an old station wagon, carpooling to school. As we thought of the recesses and the orange juice to come, gleefully we sang our silly little anthem: "We're blasting off to Blastingames!"

WILLIAM WALTON

William Walton grew up on a ranch in the Texas Hill Country. He graduated from Bandera Texas High School, then from Yale University. His stories have been published in several anthologies. His collected fiction is available in *Madmen and Fellow Travelers*.

Or Even What Kind of Ship It Was

Casey was very drunk. He leaned his forearms on the cold, sticky stern rail and hung his head over the side. The sea was rough, and every time the ship rolled so did his stomach. His drink sloshed over, soaking his wrist and sleeve, but none of this distracted him from the memory of stone-faced mortuary people, condolences from friends, his wife in a body bag, nights alone, and whiskey—lots of whiskey.

Casey stared down into the dark turbulence of the ship's prop wash, its trailing wake beckoning him. It would be so easy...

Shaken by his dark impulse, he jerked upright and gripped the railing hard with his free hand. He struggled to gather himself, to erase all memory, all thought.

As the ship plowed through the night roiling Casey's stomach, the lights of another ship came into view. Casey felt strangely warmed by the lights of this passing vessel, even though the night was too dark and it was too far away to tell its name or even what kind of ship it was.

At least it has a destination, he thought. That's worth something.

His sickness and despair eased, and all night he gazed into the blackness hoping to see the lights of still another ship that, if sighted, would pass from view just as surely and swiftly as the one before.

Embracing his solitude, Casey was soothed by the sound of the water rushing below.

Just before dawn, an over-friendly passenger found him, very hung over, still at the railing, the warm remnants of his drink in his hand.

"Up a bit early aren't you?" asked the passenger, a big, imposing man.

"No, actually I'm up late," replied Casey, looking up at him.

"Howdy. My name is—"

"I don't care what your name is." Casey turned his gaze back to the water.

"Let's try again. What's your damned name?"

"Casey to my friends, but you're not one of them."

"Friendly son of a bitch, aren't you?"

"Yeah, well, you got it half right."

"Hey, listen. We got off on the wrong foot. How about we start over? This is my first cruise. How about you?"

"Please just leave me—"

"My wife, Molly, and I think it's great. Our favorite spot so far is Cozumel. We plan to go back and learn to dive. Molly always says—"

"Look, I don't want to talk, okay? I'm looking for ships."

"I don't see any ships."

"There aren't any right now, but there will be."

"I think you're wasting your time."

Casey turned and faced the man. "No, you are wasting my time."

"And you are really being an asshole," the man replied, his eyes narrowing.

"You know, you're absolutely right. How would you like to go down to C deck and have some breakfast?"

"Fine idea," the man replied, relaxing.

"Good. Why don't you go have some then" Casey suggested, "and leave me the hell alone."

"No. I think I'll kick your scrawny ass instead."

"Look, why don't we just play a nice friendly game of 'toss 'em into the sea'?"

"And just what is that?" The man asked, balling his fists.

"I think it's self-explanatory. We try to toss each other over the rail and into the water. One of us goes for a swim and the other goes for a drink. My drink could use replenishing. So could I. Works out for me either way."

"You're one crazy son of a bitch. Good thing I'm in a good mood or your ass would be shark bait. I'm going to give you a pass. Consider yourself damned fortunate."

"Not playing isn't an option. I just hope I don't spill what's left of my drink," Casey replied, stepping back slightly, turning sideways toward the man.

"You're a nut case. This is over nothing."

"No it's not. I am looking for a ship. It's over everything."

"I'm having no part of this, you sick son of a bitch." The man's fists un-balled and he moved back a step.

"Okay. I'm going to give you a pass," said Casey. "Consider yourself damned lucky. Turns out the game is optional after all."

Maybe for me as well, he thought.

The man moved quickly away. Just as he disappeared from sight Casey shouted after him, "Say hello to Molly for me." The man did not reply. And do it for yourself, man, thought Casey, every chance you get.

Casey remained at the rail until full daylight, hoping to see another ship. None came into view.

The next night found him standing at the railing again, but this time on the side deck of the ship, not at the stern. The moon, which the night before had been shrouded by clouds, tonight cast a silvery glow to the sea.

If only I could see a ship tonight, he wished.

He did not see a ship that night. There are, however, nights when Casey does see ships. He lives for those nights.

WILLIAM MAYS

William Mays is a writer/photographer and the editor of the Corpus Christi Writers series. His second book of nature photos, *Another View from Oso Creek*, will be available soon. His novel, *George: The Early Years,* is a satiric take on mafia novels. *George: The Lost Year*, another book in *The Saga of George* series, is also available. *George: The Final Days* will be available in 2022.

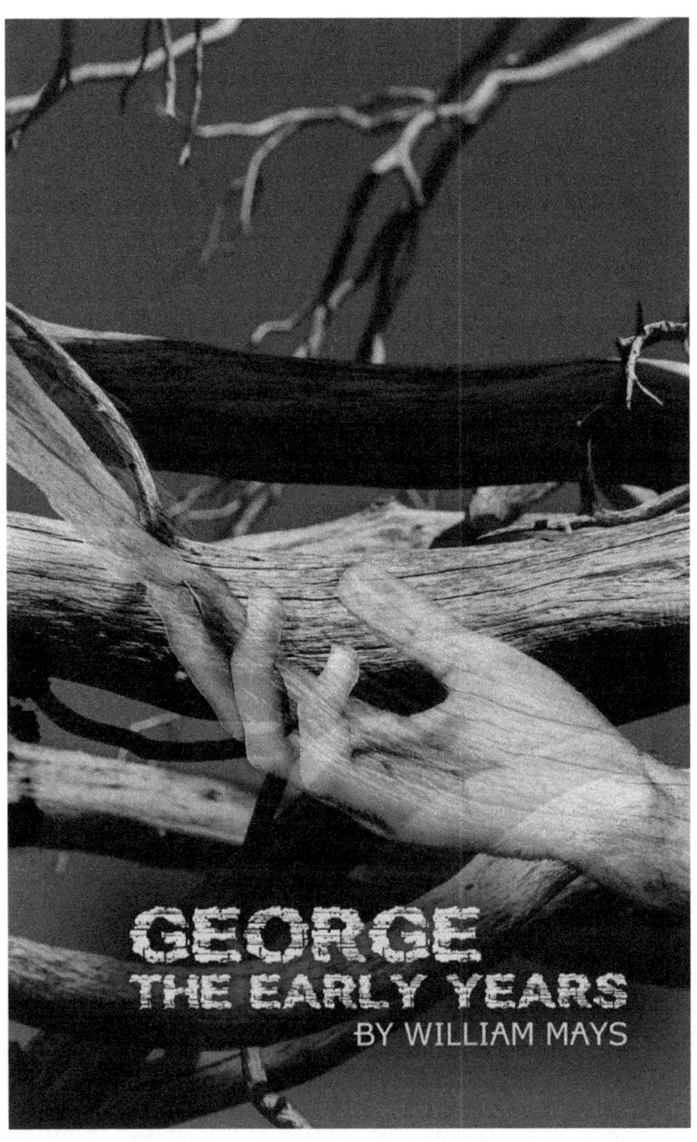

They needed to stop for gas, but he wanted to wait for a little while so they wouldn't look so stoned. The music pulsed from the tinny speaker on the radio, a rock-and-roll station in country-music land.

Time drifted with the songs, and when he rechecked the gas gauge, it was way past one-quarter, closing in on E. They had to stop soon, real soon. There was road construction ahead. A bulldozer pushed gravel and asphalt into a pile, churning up a cloud of dust. It swirled around them, making it hard to see. A worker waved a yellow flag to slow them down. A red bandana covered the bottom half of his face.

George couldn't see the road with all the swirling dust but finally spotted a sliver of cracked asphalt veering to the right. He drove down it as the worker waved his flag and yelled.

"I wonder what he wants?" George said, looking back.

Kelly's head was drooping, but she jerked awake. "What?"

"That worker."

She looked back. "He's waving at us."

"I guess maybe I was supposed to stop."

They left the large cloud behind but had barely gotten past it when he saw that the asphalt had ended, and they were on a gravel road. She grabbed hold of the armrest when they hit a big rock. "Where are we?"

"I don't know. I just followed the road. I thought I was on the highway."

She looked at all the empty desert around them. "There are no other cars." Her voice had a sharp edge to it, a burr that caught in the hot air. "Don't you think there would be cars? Or road signs?"

"I'm sure we'll hit a paved section soon," he said, trying to sound confident even as doubt crept up inside him.

They kept bouncing along, and the road grew rougher instead of smoother. There were no cars, no road signs, and the construction cloud was a blip far behind them and receding from view.

The gas gauge moved closer to E.

"Maybe I took a wrong turn?"

She looked at him with one eye cocked.

The road grew narrower; it no longer seemed like a road. *Path* or *trail* seemed like a better label, and then modifiers and clichés became necessary. *Unmarked trail. Unmaintained path. Long-abandoned road.* Finally, though, it became indistinguishable from the rocky land around it. It lost its identity as a means of getting from one point to the other. It merged with the cosmos. It was a metaphor. They had taken a difficult path, and the farther they went, the more their options narrowed. A sense of doom settled over him.

A rocky escarpment jutted sharply upward in front of them, blocking their path. He stopped and hiked to the top. It was a steep incline;

twenty percent was his guess. The rocks crunched and crumbled under his feet. Occasionally his boots slipped, and he struggled to maintain his footing. The hot air swirled around him, picking up dust that got in his eyes and nose and mouth. The sun rose in the pale cloudless sky. A horsefly, probably the only living thing in this little corner of hell, bedeviled him all the way up.

When he reached the top, he shielded his face with one hand and swatted at the fly with the other while looking for a road ahead. Nothing. Only desolation. Rock punctuated by cactus. That left only one option. They had to go back. He turned to look in the direction from which they'd come. No path. Where had it gone? How could it disappear? He rubbed his eyes and looked again. Nothing. Sure, he was stoned all to hell, but he couldn't have imagined that there had been a road, even though it hadn't been much of a road.

It was the vagaries of perception, he decided. From his vantage point on the ground, there had been a road, but there was no visible road from this summit, as cities might disappear if viewed from space. However, he could navigate by the dust cloud from the construction site. It would stand out. He scanned the horizon. Alas, it too was gone. Was it too far to be seen, or had they stopped working, taken a lunch break, and the dust had settled down?

They would run out of gas in this purgatory and die of thirst, their sun-bleached bones eventually found by roadbuilders or geologists or some other lost souls.

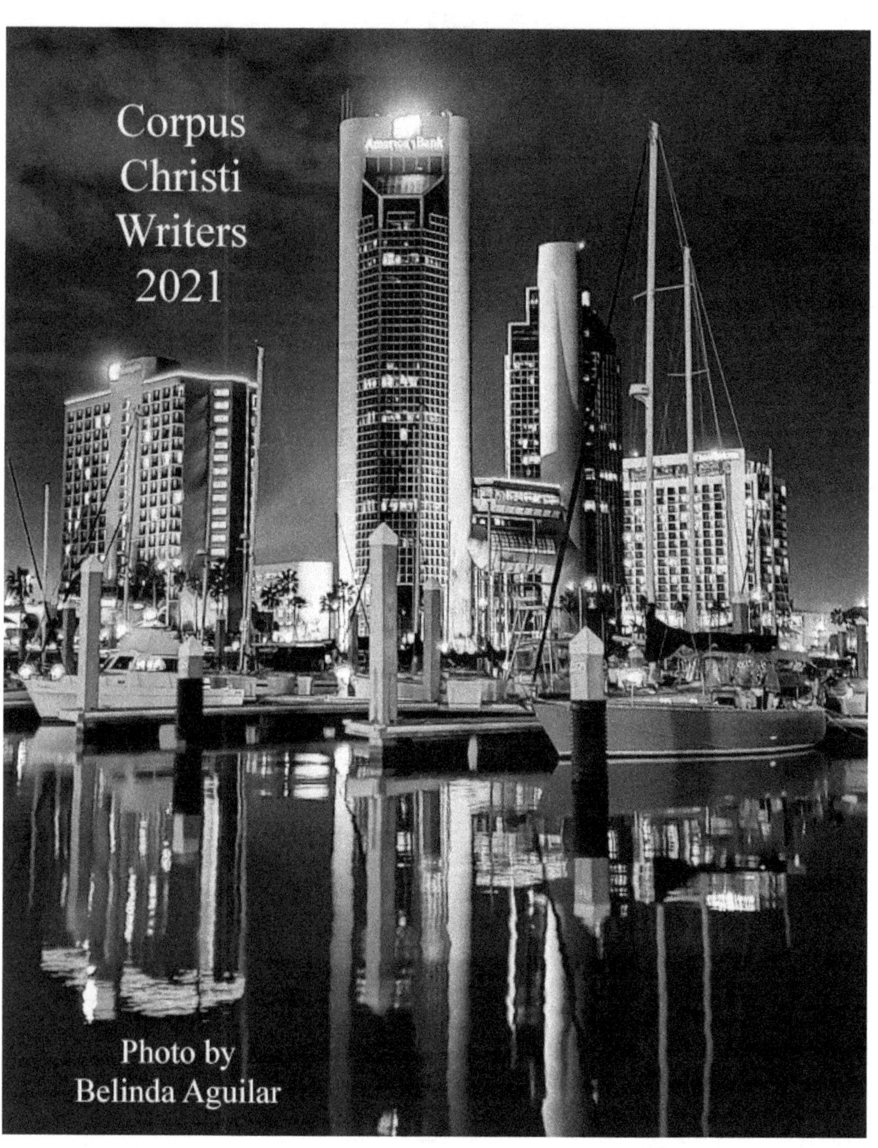
Corpus
Christi
Writers
2021
Photo by
Belinda Aguilar

ZER

ZER :3 (Zoe Elise Ramos) is a multi-modal poet and talking cat from Corpus Christi. They are slowly earning a Master's, studying English and whatever the hell they want at TAMU-CC. Their research and poetry is intertwined by necessity because art fills gaps in knowledge that would be imperceptible otherwise. They hope to bring more interest in genre-bending, interdisciplinary and humanistic research and learning models. They are the Senior Editor of *Windward Review* creative journal and blog. www.windwardreview.com

What does it take

to get to that place
and still know
the real you?

tapered, skimped peeling off
from the teeth guts falling out guts falling
out why wont you die ?

the first
memoriesinnocencesin
obscurefutile efforts of becoming,

becoming becoming what? at war with
the nothingness, insensible sensibility
incapability of expressing

what thou whilst.
she didn't know what to say
just be careful where you step
not today not today.

remember i was young
and we used to watch rated r movies
together like what all the world said
about profanity, parenting meant
nothing, mother

when a sex scene came on, mother
you would tell us to look away,
older sister and me only 9 or 10.
we would giggle and think little of it
the moaning the gasping the feverish
way you would want us to fail to see
pixels on a screen in oscillating colors
red blue green
colors i once knew
that i now know are struck
into a brain electronically
imaginationorgans sensory pressures,
body saying what things are
before you do
eyes turn over, there are always
mistakes

where people love you

Here's this trouble, she always thought too much of me. i am a
bug-utterchaos entrails with no anatomy
that's ever been known

the worse animals are immortal seeming just wont die

i was 21 years old when i told my mother that i was dating, the first human being i had ever dated, someone without gender, but black white black and white black white black white black white or another 'comprehensible' 'color'.   the selfishness,

what i did

the selfishness

e very thing

no. i was dating what parents would call a woman. shield your eyes

a girl-thing that knew themself better than themself. i don't blame you for your anger

LAtERALRebuke

What does it take
to get to that place **where people love you**
and still know
the real you?

Here's this trouble, she always thought too much of me. **i** am
a bug-utterchaos entrails with no anatomy
that's ever been known

tapered, skimped peeling off from
the teeth guts falling out guts falling
out why wont you die ?

the worse animals are immortal seeming just wont die

the first
memoriesinnocencesin
obscurefutile efforts of becoming,

becoming becoming what? at war with
the nothingness, insensible sensibility
incapability of expressing

i was 21 years old when i told my mother that i was dating
the first humanbeing i had ever dated, one without gender but
black white black and white black white black white-black-
white or another 'comprehensible' 'color', the selfishness,
what i did

what thou whilst.
she didn't know what to say
just be careful where you step
not today not today.

You couldn't h av e the com mon de cency,
the th ought ful ness to hide Your Self from
Me? I hid every thi n g from my Par en ts!
EVERYTHING

no. i was dating what parents would call a woman.
shield your eyes

remember i was young
and we used to watch rated r movies
together like what all the world said
about profanity, parenting meant
nothing, mother

a girl-thing that knew themself better than themself.
i don't blame you for your anger

when a sex scene came on, mother
you would tell us to look away,
older sister and me only 9 or 10.
we would giggle and think little of it
the moaning the gasping the feverish
way you would want us to fail to see
pixels on a screen in oscillating colors
red blue green
colors i once knew
that i now know are struck
into a brain electronically
imaginationorgans sensory pressures,
body saying what things are
before you do
eyes turn over, there are always
mistakes

It's j ust th at now I ha ve no rea son to
live, kn ew you w ere crazy knew you were
cr acki ng. I kn ew noth ing good cou ld hap pen
for us. CURSED. I gu ess I ha ve
no reas on to live

ALL PossiBilities
ARE IMPOSSIBLE in SOME PARALLEL UNIVERSE
Instanced upon yourself, You don't care
about ANY THING, EXCEPT what You care ABOUT
I know this NOW